Effective Forms of Environmental Diplomacy

This book holistically covers the issue of environmental diplomacy by building a firm foundation for readers to understand the different dimensions of the topic.

The book begins by exploring the progress the world community has made in understanding the importance of diplomacy in preserving the environment for humankind's survival, peace, and security. Then, it critically analyses the existing system of international environmental treaties and highlights its political and legal gaps. It further examines specific case studies on multilateral diplomacy as well as both formal and informal diplomacy in cases from Europe and the United States to evaluate the diplomatic models followed by different stakeholders in the field. Through this case study analysis, the book develops theoretical and empirical frameworks that can be applied to study how international and regional organisations and NGOs maintain and put forward environmental agendas at an international level. It also examines the effect of the COVID-19 pandemic on the environment to highlight the challenges to reach an effective and equitable environmental governance and draw conclusions around effective versus ineffective forms and tools of environmental diplomacy.

This book will be of great interest to students and scholars of environmental diplomacy and environmental law and governance, as well as practitioners working in this important field.

Leila Nicolas, PhD, is Professor of International Relations at the Lebanese University in Beirut and Lebanese Army Staff and Command Academy. She is the founder of the NGO "Lebanese for Democracy and Good Governance" and has 21 years of civil society experience in conflict resolution, peace-building, justice, and the rule of law. As a MENA expert, Dr. Nicolas writes weekly political articles and serves as an expert commentator for several media outlets. She is an author of eight Arabic books on contemporary international relations, Great Powers' politics, and grand strategies and MENA politics. Her book, *The Arab World in Transition: The Rough Road to Justice*, was published in 2020.

Elie Kallab is Deputy Project Lead for the Local Pathways Fellowship at UN Sustainable Development Solutions Network-Youth. He is a graduate and member committee of research and valorisation for the Oeil sur la Cite blog for Sciences Po Aix (Institute of Political Studies) in France. Elie has Master's degree in Conflict Management and Humanitarian Action from the University of Siena in Italy. He is equally a member of the steering committee for a research school on mobilisation and gender; *CORMED*. Elie has co-authored a book chapter in *Harness It: Renewable Energy Technologies and Project Development Models Transforming the Grid*.

Routledge Focus on Environment and Sustainability

Post-Pandemic Sustainable Tourism Management
The New Reality of Managing Ethical and Responsible Tourism
Tony O'Rourke and Marko Koščak

Consumption Corridors
Living a Good Life within Sustainable Limits
Doris Fuchs, Marlyne Sahakian, Tobias Gumbert, Antonietta Di Giulio, Michael Maniates, Sylvia Lorek and Antonia Graf

The Ecological Constitution
Reframing Environmental Law
Lynda Collins

Effective Forms of Environmental Diplomacy
Leila Nicolas and Elie Kallab

Coastal Wetlands Restoration
Public Perception and Community Development
Edited by Hiromi Yamashita

Sustainability in High-Excellence Italian Food and Wine
Laura Onofri

Learning to Live with Climate Change
From Anxiety to Transformation
Blanche Verlie

For more information about this series, please visit: www.routledge.com/Routledge-Focus-on-Environment-and-Sustainability/book-series/RFES

Effective Forms of Environmental Diplomacy

Leila Nicolas and Elie Kallab

LONDON AND NEW YORK

First published 2021
by Routledge
2 Park Square, Milton Park, Abingdon, Oxon OX14 4RN

and by Routledge
605 Third Avenue, New York, NY 10158

Routledge is an imprint of the Taylor & Francis Group, an informa business

© 2021 Leila Nicolas and Elie Kallab

The right of Leila Nicolas and Elie Kallab to be identified as authors of this work has been asserted by them in accordance with sections 77 and 78 of the Copyright, Designs and Patents Act 1988.

All rights reserved. No part of this book may be reprinted or reproduced or utilised in any form or by any electronic, mechanical, or other means, now known or hereafter invented, including photocopying and recording, or in any information storage or retrieval system, without permission in writing from the publishers.

Trademark notice: Product or corporate names may be trademarks or registered trademarks, and are used only for identification and explanation without intent to infringe.

British Library Cataloguing-in-Publication Data
A catalogue record for this book is available from the British Library

Library of Congress Cataloging-in-Publication Data
Names: Nicolas, Leila, author. | Kallab, Elie, author.
Title: Effective forms of environmental diplomacy / Leila Nicolas and Elie Kallab.
Description: Milton Park, Abingdon, Oxon ; New York, NY : Routledge, 2022. | Series: Routledge focus on environment and sustainability | Includes bibliographical references and index.
Subjects: LCSH: Environmental protection—International cooperation. | Environmental policy—International cooperation. | Environmental law, International.
Classification: LCC HC79.E5 N465 2022 (print) | LCC HC79.E5 (ebook) | DDC 363.7/056—dc23
LC record available at https://lccn.loc.gov/2021012347
LC ebook record available at https://lccn.loc.gov/2021012348

ISBN: 978-0-367-47163-7 (hbk)
ISBN: 978-1-032-06966-1 (pbk)
ISBN: 978-1-003-03386-8 (ebk)

Typeset in Times New Roman
by Apex CoVantage, LLC

Contents

List of case studies vi
Acknowledgements vii
List of abbreviations viii

1 Environmental diplomacy evolution: an introduction 1

2 Legal and political dimensions of International Environmental Law 12

3 Environmental issues at international and regional levels: informal diplomacy 25

4 Towards a more effective environmental governance 40

5 Conclusion: the need for environmental diplomats 55

Index 60

Case studies

4.1 COVID-19 pandemic and the environment: opportunities
     amid disasters *Tatiana Rahbany*   41
4.2 Multilateral diplomacy: forest conservation   51
5.1 Environmental diplomacy through technical training at
     US embassies *Michael Ginsberg*   55

Acknowledgements

We want to express our gratitude to all our colleagues and friends who reviewed, gave comments, shared their views and insights, and remained directly or indirectly with us in our journey to complete this book. Special thanks to Andrea Gallinal Arias and Guillemette Lano, for their input to the Chapter 3 of the book. We would also thank Routledge team for their patience and relentless support.

We particularly want to thank Tatiana Rahbany and Michael Ginsberg for sharing their expertise and for their generous contribution by adding extensive knowledge to this book through their insightful case studies.

Abbreviations

CFC	Chlorofluorocarbons
CSD	United Nations Commission on Sustainable Development
EEB	European Environmental Bureau
ENGO	Environmental non-governmental organisation
IEL	International Environmental Law
IGO	International governmental organization
IPCC	Intergovernmental Panel on Climate Change
MDG	Millennium Development Goals
NGO	Non-governmental organization
UNCED	United Nation Conference on Environment and Development
UNCLOS	United Nations Convention on the Law of the Sea
UNCSD	United Nations Conference on Sustainable Development
UNEP	United Nations Environment Program
UNFCCC	United Nations Framework Convention on Climate Change
UNSDSN	United Nations Sustainable Development Solutions Network
WCED	World Commission on Environment and Development
WHO	World Health Organization

1 Environmental diplomacy evolution
An introduction

Diplomacy

States have practised diplomacy since the formation of the first city-states and even earlier than that. The Greek word "diploma" is the origin of diplomacy.

In the eighteenth century, the French language adopted the word "*diplomate*" referring to a statesman authorised to negotiate and deal with other states (Freeman & Marks, 2018). Later on, the word "diplomacy" spread to all languages, and now it merely refers to "the profession, activity, or skill of managing international relations, typically by a state's representatives abroad" (Oxford University Press, 2018). Diplomacy has always evolved and advanced, conforming to the emerging needs of states.

Traditional diplomacy

Some would describe the institution of diplomacy as "old as history itself" (Sen, 1965). Usually, diplomats enrol in negotiations to preserve peaceful and cooperative relations between states and sometimes avoid hostilities. The Greeks initially developed the basis of the European tradition of diplomacy.

Europeans inherited the practice and developed it. The Romans adopted the early form of diplomacy to satisfy imperial administration needs, establishing a department for foreign affairs for the first time in history (Freeman & Marks, 2018). Spain set a precedent by sending a permanent representative to the Court of England in 1487, which became the international standard norm later on. The first to professionally train diplomats were the Byzantines, who were coached into espionage and collecting information. These diplomatic customs lived long after the Byzantine Empire's downfall (Freeman & Marks, 2018).

Following the Roman Empire, the Roman Catholic Church added new practices, such as "plenipotentiaries" who had been given the discretionary

2 *Environmental diplomacy evolution*

authority to negotiate and sign treaties on behalf of their sovereigns. In the twelfth century, Italy commissioned "*ambassadors*" who carried a letter of credence with limited authorities to act as sovereign.

After the industrial revolution, established norms and customs of diplomatic relations were described by Grotius: "there are two maxims in the law of nations relating to Ambassadors which are generally accepted as established rules: the first is that Ambassadors must be received, and the second is that they must suffer no harm" (Grotius, 1901).

According to B. Sen, the balance of power was one of the main reasons why the last decades of the seventeenth century saw a willingness to establish permanent diplomatic missions among states, to "keep an eye or sneak" on one another, and since diplomatic envoys were to be received and were inviolable – as Grotius stated – permanent diplomatic missions were the appropriate tool. By the nineteenth century, the world adopted European-style permanent missions and foreign ministries' systems.

After signing the treaty of Westphalia, diplomacy and the state system evolved together, both in the service of new states' personal and national interests. However, since most diplomats were aristocrats – and secretive, European diplomacy was elitist, which meant that it separated the ordinary citizen from foreign policy, making it a state-to-state only diplomacy (Younger, 1964).

States continuously tried to regulate diplomatic practices to solve disputes peacefully, beginning mainly after the Congress of Vienna (1815). Nevertheless, the First and Second World Wars revealed that diplomacy could not prevent military escalations and colonialist competition from leading states to war. It was until the "Vienna Convention on Diplomatic Relations" 1961 that government-to-government diplomacy was regulated.

Contemporary developments of diplomacy

Today, diplomacy is facing many challenges that require better practices. It has had to realise the urgency to evolve or perish. Thus, traditional diplomacy has been forced to change to fit the needs of the twenty-first century.

Since the end of the Cold War, diplomacy has witnessed a transformation in practitioners' expertise; an increased number of states and new actors flourished alongside states internationally.

Non-state actors played significant roles as international governmental organisations (IGOs), non-governmental organisations (NGOs), and even multinational corporations. The multiplicity of actors on the international level, with different roles and impacts, lead to "multilateral diplomacy".

The international order can no longer be preserved through the harmonious cooperation between states, especially since continuous and sound communication, utilising modern mediums, is now needed between states and between state and other players like non-state actors (Younger, 1964). Those actors often had a critical eye harmful to states' images and foreign policy practices.

The fact that IGOs are inefficient on their own does not mean that they are not beneficial to their member-states. These organisations ultimately serve traditional diplomacy in enhancing bilateral and multilateral diplomacy between sovereign states. What is notable is that they gave states, non-state actors, and regional organisations a voice and a medium to interact.

In turn, this voice allowed more people to become cognizant of their national, regional, and international circumstances, and with this awareness came the need to be heard. Thus, public opinion began to transcend national boundaries and manipulate international forums, drawing the attention and the interest of states and non-state actors alike.

These developments are proof that changes in the practice of diplomacy were not only required but also present; states were beginning to feel more like a community, increasingly appreciating the weight carried by public opinion – both nationally and internationally – and benefit from the rapid increase in communication technologies at that time (Nicolson, 1964).

Many scholars believe this to be true, including Brian Hocking. He believes that the breakthrough of diplomacy as non-traditional – meaning no longer limited to government-to-government diplomacy – reflects the augmentation of the diplomatic agenda to adopt issues such as human rights, human security, and the environment. It also strengthens the capacity of NGOs to operate alongside governments on the international level, challenging the latter's authority (Hocking, 1999).

Whereas government officials or individuals acting in an official capacity conduct traditional diplomacy, directly with the other states' representative and away more-or-less from the public eye, public diplomacy engages with people first and foremost, on different levels and through various channels. This development has made diplomats more visible than they have ever been.

Therefore, public diplomacy can be defined as an "instrument used by states, communities of states, and non-state actors taking into consideration their understanding of civilisations, cultures, attitudes, and behaviours, to maintain relationships, influence public opinion, and mobilise actions to advance their interests" (Gregory, 2011).

The environment in diplomatic relations

Being a state-centric practice, diplomacy in its early traditional sense focused only on "high politics", i.e. national security, defence, and sovereignty,

4 *Environmental diplomacy evolution*

and did not weigh what was considered "low politics", i.e. social, cultural, environmental issues which were considered peripheral. Despite starting to negotiate environmental treaties in the mid-nineteenth century, it was not until states began to view the environment as a threat to security that they began to practice effective environmental diplomacy.

Climate-related security concerns were water and food security, oceans and sea-level rise, climate change, migration, and environment-related conflicts. Since then, the environment has entered the realm of "high politics".

Lester Brown was the first to link the environment to national security and coin the term "environmental security". In his seminal publication in 1977, he wrote, "the threats to security may now arise less from a relationship of nation to nation and more from the relationship of man to nature" (Brown, 1977).

"Environmental security" is a modern, rapidly growing field relevant to resource scarcity and its conflicts in the developing world. Not only was it labelled a national security issue, but also a global security issue. Some argue that the rising demand for natural resources, particularly energy, is one of the most significant security challenges of the twenty-first century (Kay, 2015).

Whether through the availability of resources, climate change, or other environmental issues, this linkage between man and nature has become embedded in politics and business. In the early twenty-first century, with the media approaching environmental issues with alarm and panic, consumers and particularly younger generations are opting for more eco-conscious products, with a rise in recycling practices and awareness to waste management and environmental issues.

Scarcity or abundance of natural resources may cause environmental conflict in a particular region. Those who are threatened are the vulnerable communities at the local level and the state at a broader level. Some argue that resources are not the cause of conflict, rather "amplifiers" of already-existing tensions.

Historically, security involved threats to the physical safety and survival of a target by a purposeful attacker. It included the study of the elements that make a target possible or attractive, and the target's vulnerabilities.

Following the end of the Cold War, the term "security" has been altered by scholars' linkage to various concepts. The term "environmental conflict" refers to a violent conflict over natural resources. These conflicts may threaten human beings (environmental security) and the environment itself (ecological security).

Environmental conflicts' narratives

In his address to the Security Council, on 23 February 2021, the UN Secretary General António Guterres warned "where climate change dries up

rivers, reduces harvest, destroys critical infrastructure, and displaces communities, it exacerbates the risks of instability and conflict"
Environmental conflict is portrayed differently by scholars. Each region has its perspectives on the threats associated with environmental degradation. These perspectives stem from the actors' positions, geopolitical, and environmental contexts.

Natural resource scarcity

Some are preoccupied with resource availability concerns. Many believe that natural resource scarcity threatening some regions is a significant contributor to the outbreak of violence and political conflict. Homer-Dixon identified "three types of scarcities: supply-induced scarcity, demand-induced scarcity, and structural scarcity" (Homer-Dixon, 2010). The first and the second are caused by a decrease in supply and an increase in demand. Simultaneously, structural scarcity is the change in access to a key resource by one party or the other.

The causal relationship between resource scarcity and conflicts has not been definitively verified. Examining this relationship within East and West Africa conflicts showed that "resource scarcity is never the most important cause and it does not explain well the differences in conflict intensity" (Seter et al., 2018). Nevertheless, this relationship must be studied on a case-by-case basis. In the Syrian conflict, for example, environmental resource scarcity was one factor that fuelled the insurgence against the State. However, many other and, more significant, contextual factors have led to the Civil War in Syria, such as the regional balance of power, sectarianism, dictatorship, and international interference.

Population growth

Another narrative relating to environmental conflict is the concerns of population size. Never in history have humans been concerned to this extent with their number and their effect on their environment. The rationale surrounding this narrative is that the more the humans exist, the more they are likely to engage in conflict over resources. The argument is that "continued human population growth will eventually ruin both humans and the environment" (Hardin, 1968).

Population growth is also a concern for those adopting the youth bulge's narrative, which means the massive number of young people in a society should be a cause for concern. It has been linked to the conflict in several manners, especially in the presence of poor economic performance (Urdal, 2004). The population size narrative yields no definitive causal relationship. However, according to Urdal (2004), human migration "acts as a safety valve" for conflict, reducing youth tension in economic recessions.

Human migration

Human migration is yet another narrative of environmental conflict. The argument is that "once people are forced to migrate due to a lack of resources, conflicts will arise, and group-identity issues could lead to violence" (Martin, 2005). Once a migrant community is displaced due to environmental degradation, existing social, economic, or political tensions are aggravated within migrant and host societies and possible conflicts may arise over host resources. Those who relate to this narrative usually believe that several factors are likely to cause environmental conflict, rather than resource scarcity per se.

Globalisation

The globalisation narrative also emerged in the environmental conflict discourse. Some groups have believed themselves to be more advanced than others. Globalisation has threatened those perceptions by destroying economic, cultural, and social borders (Gare, 2006).

Ho-Won Jeong (2001) maintains that environmental conflict has been globalised and regionalised, and its nature reflects an asymmetric relationship between victims and polluters (Jeong, 2001).

This narrative also relates to the concept of food security, where globalisation has allowed for mass production and distribution, often at the expense of one region (McDonald, 2010). Food insecurity could be the result of unequal resource distribution rather than the shortage of food.

Unequal resource distribution

Unequal resource distribution is another narrative of environmental conflict. Some regions are more resourceful than others, leading to an imbalance in society. The exploitation of some states of others' resources is not uncommon. Conflict results from "the unequal distribution of outcomes arising from environmental degradation and the processes that cause it" (Walton & Barnett, 2008). When communities experience livelihood insecurity due to environmental degradation, the disadvantaged members of society will suffer the most, and as a result, violence will likely emerge.

Environmental diplomacy: a peace-building tool

Environmental conflicts, regardless of the narrative, pose new challenge for states' foreign policies. The relationship between environmental security and peace-building started with the concept of "sustainable peace", which emerged in the 1990s. Since then, environmental peace-building has advanced through four scientific exploration waves, followed by similar environmental-conflict research waves (Hardt & Scheffran, 2019).

According to (Kalinowski, 2012) environmental peace-building studies are getting lost between human poverty, human security, and development studies. Thus, some argue that scholars must study peace-building separately from violence and conflict (Dalby, 2018; Swatuk, 2018). Scholars are urging policymakers to create sustainable policies in response to environmental risks, based on concepts that facilitate collaboration and mutual understanding (Mobjörk, 2017).

"Environmental diplomacy" in international affairs refers to the negotiations held by different players, mainly states, on environmental governance. In practice, states must engage in environmental diplomacy based on cooperation, preventive diplomacy, conflict resolution, and peacemaking. As established earlier, environmental issues can affect the livelihood and economic security, acting as threat multipliers, creating difficulties for trade exchange and economy for states in conflict areas.

"Environmental diplomacy" falls under two categories: conventions regulating natural resources and those regulating pollution. The problem is that states' territorial boundaries rarely reflect natural boundaries, so national industries and consumption devastate resources and generate pollution causing environmental problems beyond the state.

The economy and environment are interconnected. Environmental diplomacy will not succeed without considering economic interests. Besides, economic diplomacy will not be sustainable unless it addresses environmental issues.

The "United Nations Environment Program" (UNEP) provides an excellent groundwork for combating environmental issues, and recommends nations to integrate environmental issues into their negotiations, rather than treating them as independent matters (UNEP, 2016).

Negotiating on nature

Depending on their interests, states can have three types of negotiations. Sharing the same interests leads government officials to meet and discuss at a round table in order to set a common strategy. Whereas having conflicting interests makes negotiations inevitable. The most complicated case is when the states have both shared and opposing interests. Negotiation, in this case, is an effective means of conflict resolution.

Usually, internal conflicts over economic versus environmental policies cause a disturbance in the state's negotiating power and weaken it, giving opposing parties an advantage, albeit states or IGOs.

The proliferation of IGOs has changed environmental diplomacy from a simple, bilateral relationship to a complex, multilateral one. IGOs can have a large role in state negotiations and states' relationships with non-state actors, causing diplomacy to involve hundreds of different governmental and non-governmental participants (Karns et al., 2015)

IGOs and civil societies have enacted new norms and pressured states to abide by the universal principles of respecting human rights, protecting the environment, and affecting states' relations with their citizens.

Informal groups have altered the way of conducting international negotiations, especially on the environment. Despite not having an official status, coalitions between states or NGOs facilitate coordination between these groups and lead to unanimous group situations. Coalition-building is a form of "associative diplomacy" (Melissen, 1999) that serves to increase the group members' bargaining strength when voting and increase lobbying power. A noticeable example is the EU Green Diplomacy Network

Coalition negotiation reduces negotiation efforts, as the number of speakers at a convention increases the negotiators' effectiveness. Nevertheless, negotiating as a group can also provide limited flexibility and hinder agreements when group members are not harmonious, and when member interests do not overlap totally.

Topics discussed in this chapter serve as an introduction for the following chapters of this book.

Chapter 2 discusses the role of "International Environmental Law" in the inclusion of environment in the international and regional political agenda. It starts with the definition of related concepts, and then elaborates on the historical development of the designated law. Environmental law history can be classified into four generations. Each generation mirrors the political and scientific contexts and the ability of the actors to push the "green agenda" forward. This chapter sets off with the IEL principles, current weaknesses, and challenges, i.e. compliance, enforcement, and implementation.

Chapter 3 analyses the role of informal diplomacy, i.e. lobbying and advocacy, practised by ENGOs to promote nature. Discussing informal diplomacy, this chapter covers ENGOs' role, particularly their lobbying campaigns vis-à-vis the European political sphere. It also investigates the various lobbying, advocacy strategies, and repertory actions classified as

"Brussels ENGOs" and "Non-Brussels ENGOs". Three case studies had been discussed: Green Peace, European Environmental Bureau, and the UN Sustainable Development Solutions Network.

Chapter 4 discusses how to move forward toward a better environmental governance, which pushes different stakeholders to sit and negotiate nature. This chapter highlights the definition and key principles of environmental governance, in addition to environmental policy priority areas. It illustrates the many challenges facing environmental governance at the international and national levels, and tries to give some reform recommendations to ensure effective, equitable, responsive, and robust environmental governance.

Two related case studies have been discussed at the end of Chapter 4:

> Tatiana Rahbany discusses in Case Study 4.1 the effects of the coronavirus pandemic on the environment and quality of life. She explains, as well, the relationship between healthcare spending, environment, and economic growth.
>
> Case Study 4.2 discusses the effectiveness of multilateral diplomacy through the area of forest conservation. Within forest negotiations, efforts of state actors, scientists, experts, and civil society organisations resulted in the recognition of inequitable land tenure pattern in the forest convention.

In the conclusion, Michael Ginsberg (Case Study 5.1) gives his insights and experience in environmental training for the US diplomats. Then, we conclude by providing an advisory framework for expert diplomats to engage environment in high politics. The conclusion progressively skims through some of the formal and informal diplomatic training programmes organised by governments and private organisations to show the advantages, gaps, and challenges facing such programmes.

Bibliography

Brown, L., 1977. *Redefining National Security*. Washington, DC: World Watch Institute.
Dalby, S., 2018. Climate Change and Environmental Conflicts. In Ashok Swain & Joakim Öjendal, eds. *Routledge Handbook of Environmental Conflict and Peacebuilding*. Abingdon: Routledge, pp. 42–53.
Freeman, C. & Marks, S., 2018. *Diplomacy*. [Online] Encyclopedia Britannica. Available at: www.britannica.com/topic/diplomacy [Accessed 5 June 2020].
Gare, A., 2006. *Postmodernism and the Environmental Crisis*. London: Routledge.

Gregory, B., 2011. American Public Diplomacy: Enduring Characteristics, Elusive Transformation. *The Hague Journal of Diplomacy*, 6(3–4), p. 353.

Grotius, H., 1901. *The Rights of War and Peace*. [Online] Available at: www.bartleby.com/172/218.html [Accessed 22 June 2020].

Hardin, G., 1968. The Tragedy of the Commons. *Science*, 162(3859), pp. 1243–1248.

Hardt, J. & Scheffran, J., 2019. *Environmental Peacebuilding and Climate Change: Peace and Conflict Studies at the Edge of Transformation*. Tokyo: Toda Peace Institute.

Hocking, B., 1999. Catalytic Diplomacy: Beyond Newness and Decline. In *Innovation in Diplomatic Practice*. New York: Palgrave, p. 32.

Homer-Dixon, T.F., 2010. *Environment, Scarcity, and Violence*. Princeton: Princeton University Press.

Jeong, H.W., 2001. *Global Environmental Policies: Institutions and Procedures*. 1st ed. London: Springer.

Kalinowski, M., 2012. Klimawandel und Konflikte: Was ist die Aufgabe für Friedensund Konfliktforschung?. in M. Brzoska, M. Kalinowski, M.Volker & M. Berthold, eds. *Klimawandel und Konflikte. Versicherheitlichung versus präventive Friedenspolitik?*. Hamburg: Nomos. pp. 271-284.

Karns, M.P., Mingst, K.A. & Stiles, K.W., 2015. *International Organizations:The Politics and Processes of Global Governance*. Boulder,USA: Lynne Rienner Publishers.

Kay, S., 2015. *Global Security in the Twenty-First Century: The Quest for Power and the Search for Peace*. New York: Rowman & Littlefield.

Martin, A., 2005. The Environmental Conflict between Refugee and Host Communities. *Journal of peace research*, 42(3), pp. 329–346.

McDonald, B., 2010. *Food Security*. 1st ed. Cambridge: Polity Press.

Melissen, J., 1999. *Innovation in Diplomatic Practice*. New York: Palgrave.

Mobjörk, M., 2017. Exploring the Climate-Conflict Link: The Case of East Africa. In SIPRI, ed. *Armaments, Disarmament and International Security*. Oxford: Oxford University Press, pp. 287–299.

Nicolson, H., 1964. *Diplomacy*. New York: Oxford University Press.

Oxford University Press, 2018. *Diplomacy*. [Online] Available at: https://en.oxforddictionaries.com/definition/diplomacy [Accessed 5 June 2020].

Sen, B., 1965. *A Diplomat's Handbook of International Law and Practice*. The Hague: Springer.

Seter, H., Theisen, O.M. & Schilling, J., 2018. All About Water and Land? Resource-related Conflicts in East and West Africa Revisited. *GeoJournal*, 83(1), pp. 169–187.

Swatuk, L., 2018. Environmental Resource Governance and Peace. A Critical Review. In Ashok Swain & Joakim Öjendal, eds. *Routledge Handbook of Environmental Conflict and Peacebuilding*. Abingdon: Routledge, pp. 315–28.

UNEP, 2016. *Annual Report, 2015*. New York: United Nations Environment Programme.

Urdal, H., 2004. *The Devil in the Demographics: The Effect of Youth Bulges on Domestic Armed Conflict, 1950–2000*. Washington, D.C.: World Bank Group. .

Walton, G. and J. Barnett: 2008, 'The Ambiguities of "Environmental" Conflict: Insights from the Tolu- kuma Gold Mine, Papua New Guinea', *Society and Natural Resources* 21(1), 1-16.

Younger, K., 1964. Public Opinion and British Foreign Policy. *International Affairs*, 40(1), p. 22.

2 Legal and political dimensions of International Environmental Law

Defining concepts

"International Environmental Law" (IEL) is a part of public international law, drafted to minimise nature degradation, control pollution, and maintain sustainable development. It is a legal system that governs human interaction with nature and environmental systems.

It consists mainly of treaties, conventions, declarations, and protocols, in addition to other environmental customary laws. While treaties, conventions, and customary laws are legally binding, treaty laws are binding for contracting parties only. Environmental treaties can be defined as intergovernmental legally binding documents signed and ratified by states to prevent, preserve, or manage human activity consequences on natural resources (Kanie, 2007).

A convention only becomes legally binding to a state after ratification. Legally, contracting states are bound to adhere to the convention's principles. The state's implementation and adherence to the convention is usually supervised by a monitoring body that considers reports periodically submitted by States (United Nations, 2007). The "Vienna Convention for the Protection of the Ozone Layer" 1985 is one example.

Declarations are statements of intent and aspirations created by states without any binding obligations. The most important declarations in the international environmental field are the "1972 Stockholm Declaration" and the "1992 Rio Declaration".

A protocol is an agreement of a less binding nature than a treaty or convention. It is generally used to clarify, amend, or add some new rules to the original multilateral treaty. Usually, protocols are optional; it means that the contracting states to a treaty have the freedom to join the protocols or not. The "Montreal Protocol" is an example.

History

Ever since its conception five decades ago, IEL has gone through four stages of evolution. These generations reflect the advances in science and technology, diplomatic relations, and the interaction between governments, non-state actors, and international organisations. This section will outline them.

First generation: from the nineteenth century till the dawn of UN creation

This generation began with bilateral agreements between states from the first half of the nineteenth century until the creation of the United Nations. The First multilateral agreement, i.e. the "Agreement respecting the regulation of the flow of water from Lake Constance", was signed in 1857.

During this period, states usually signed limited-scope ad hoc treaties, and the creation of international environmental organisations was limited. In addition to fisheries and wildlife, preventing pollution attracted international legislators' attention, and for the first time, international tribunals looked into environmental disputes.

The judiciaries in the "Trail Smelter case" (the United States against Canada) acknowledged the principle that prevents states from causing harm to other states while exercising their right to use or giving permission to use their territory (Bratspies & Miller, 2008).

Besides, the "findings on the state of international law on air pollution" in the 1930s represented a remarkable moment for IEL development.

Second generation: UN establishment until the Stockholm Conference (1945–1972)

Two significant events marked this phase: the first was creating international and regional environmental organisations. The second was developing a global focus on pollution and its causes. The "United Nations Conference on the Conservation and Utilization of Resources" in 1949 is one example.

The "United Nations Conference on the Human Environment" held in Stockholm, Sweden, on 16 June 1972, resulted in the "Stockholm Declaration", which expressed "the urgent need to respond to the problem of environmental deterioration". Thus adopting 26 principles "urging people and governments to take their responsibility in the protection, preservation and improvement of the human environment." (United Nations, 1972)

The Stockholm Conference's most notable accomplishments were the creation of the "UN Environment Program" (UNEP) and the adoption of "Principle 21", which was a reflection of customary international law:

(a) UNEP has been responsible for forming the "Regional Seas Program", which includes over 30 regional treaties and other global treaties focusing on other environmental degradation issues like ozone depletion.

14 *Legal and political dimensions*

Moreover, more prominently, the standardisation and the monitoring and implementation of the programmes saw the participation of different international actors, including NGOs participating in the international legal process.

(b) "Article 21" assured the States' sovereign right "to exploit their resources pursuant to their environmental policies"; however, they have "the responsibility to ensure that activities within their jurisdiction or control do not cause damage to the environment of other States or of areas beyond the limits of national jurisdiction" (United Nations, 1972)

Finally, at its twenty-seventh session, the UN General Assembly adopted 11 resolutions based on the "Stockholm Conference Report", encouraging international environmental cooperation at the regional and global levels.

Third generation: post-Stockholm until the Earth Summit in Rio (1972–1992)

A considerable advance in treaty adoption characterised this period, in addition to the initiation of international environmental organisations. It was remarked by the development of international environmental laws, standards, and principles, and the integration of sustainable development and the environment in international trade treaties and resolutions (IUCN, UNEP, WWF, 2009); for example, "UNEP Draft Principles" 1978, the "Montevideo Programme" 1981, the "World Conservation Strategy" 1980, the "World Charter for Nature" 1982, and the 1991 document "Caring for the Earth: A Strategy for Sustainable Living".

One of the most significant achievements following the "Stockholm Conference" was the "United Nations Convention on the Law of the Sea" (UNCLOS) to protect marine living resources and the marine environment as a whole.

The Brundtland report "our common future," 1987

In 1983, United Nations Secretary-General Chairperson established "Brundtland Commission" to address the world's human environment and natural resources deterioration.

The "World Commission on Environment and Development" (WCED), chaired by Harlem Brundtland, issued a report titled "Our Common Future" (1987), defining "Sustainable Development" as "the development that meets the needs of the present without compromising the ability of future generations to meet their own needs" (World Commission on Environment and Development, 1987).

The report shed light on "three pillars of sustainable development: environmental protection, economic growth, and social equity. The concept of sustainable development is directed towards finding social and economic advancement that preserves the environment and avoids environmental degradation, pollution, or over-exploitation" (World Commission on Environment and Development, 1987).

Finally, perhaps the most successful global treaty relating to the environment is the "Montreal Protocol" signed in 1987. It is an international agreement aimed to preserve the Earth's ozone layer by legally phasing out certain ozone-depleting chemicals like chlorofluorocarbons (CFCs), which had been frequently used in aerosol cans.

This agreement's significance lies in its being the first environmental agreement to be signed by all 193 member states of the UN, making it a symbol of successful global cooperation in improving human health and protecting from the harmful impacts of environmental degradation.

"Earth Summit" – Rio (UNCED)

The most significant summit was the "UN Conference on Environment and Development" (UNCED), in Rio de Janeiro, Brazil, on 3–14 June 1992. It was called the "Rio Summit" or the "Earth Summit". In Rio, 154 leaders signed "The Convention on Climate Change" to "stabilise greenhouse gas concentrations in the atmosphere at a level that would prevent dangerous anthropogenic interference with the climate system" (United Nations, 1992).

The "Convention on Biological Diversity" (United Nations, 1992) was also signed during that summit. In addition to the previously mentioned treaties, three non-binding instruments have been agreed upon: The "Rio Declaration", "Agenda 21", and the "Statement of Principles for the Sustainable Management of Forests".

The "Rio Declaration on Environment and Development" was, at the time, seen as a significant shift in the States' commitment to "the recognition of the indivisibility of the fate of humankind from that of the Earth" (United Nations, 2011).

The "Rio Declaration" was more precise and detailed than "Stockholm Declaration". It addressed 27 principles of the most important environmental law principles.

"Agenda 21" was a crucial non-binding action plan to promote global, regional, and local partnerships to achieve sustainable development (UNCED, 1992).

Fourth generation: 1992

This phase focuses on sustainable development, reaffirmation, and follow-up on the environmental principles concluded in "Rio" and integrating environmental principles in global and regional actions and national policies.

It is important to note that, during this phase, the development of international law on sustainable development enhanced environmental protection. It included social and economic aspects of development, the roles of different groups in those developmental efforts, and financial and other means of implementation (UNCED, 1992).

Following the "Rio Summit", the UN General Assembly established in December 1992 the "United Nations Commission on Sustainable Development" (CSD) to follow-up on the implementation of the "Rio Declaration" and "Agenda 21".

The "Kyoto Protocol" 1997

Five years after the Rio "Earth Summit", the "Kyoto Protocol" was adopted in Kyoto, Japan, on 11 December 1997, to extend the "United Nations Framework Convention on Climate Change" (UNFCCC).

The "Kyoto Protocol" was a binding treaty that entered into force on 16 February 2005. The signatories agreed on reducing greenhouse emissions after reaching a consensus that human-made carbon dioxide emissions caused global warming.

The Protocol's first commitment period started in 2008 and was supervised periodically till its end in 2012. The evaluation of the Protocol's impact on global emissions revealed that global emissions increased by 32% from 1990 to 2010 (UNEP, 2012). Parties to "Kyoto Protocol" adopted an amendment during their meeting held in Doha, Qatar, on 8 December 2012. A total of 144 instruments of acceptance by signatories are required for the amendment to enter into force. As of 28 October 2020, 147 parties deposited their instrument of acceptance; therefore, the threshold for entry into force of the Doha Amendment was achieved. The amendment entered into force on 31 December 2020. Once in force, the emission reduction commitments of participating developed countries and economies in transition become legally binding (UNFCC, 2020).

The Millennium Development Goals (MDGs), 2000

In September 2001, based upon the General Assembly resolution 55/2 of 8 September 2000, entitled the "Millennium Declaration" (OHCHR, 2000), the United Nations submitted a list of goals, called the "Millennium

Development Goals" (MDG) to be achieved by 2015. These goals placed human development at the top of the international agenda priorities (UN, 2000).

At the end of the period, the United Nations assured that the MDGs have achieved

> the most successful anti-poverty movement in history, lifting millions out of poverty. Women gained parliamentary representation in 90% of the 174 countries. The global under-five mortality rate decreased from 90 to 43 deaths per 1,000 live births, and maternal mortality decreased by 45%, and so on.
>
> (United Nations, 2015c)

"World Summit on Sustainable Development", 2002

The "World Summit on Sustainable Development" in Johannesburg was held in South Africa, during 2–4 September 2002. Unlike Rio, which dealt with treaties and principles, "World Summit" or (Rio+10) focused primarily on implementation in sustainable development areas.

The conference succeeded in placing sustainable development on world leaders' political agenda, and tried to reinforce the Rio Principles into states' decision-making procedures and policies.

The "Johannesburg Declaration", which was the outcome of the conference, urged for a more humane and equitable global society, focusing on diminishing the conditions that may create a severe threat to the sustainable development, stressing for "more effective, democratic and accountable international and multilateral institutions" (United Nations, 2004).

(Rio+20)- "The Future We Want", 2012

The "United Nations Conference on Sustainable Development" (UNCSD), also known as Rio+20, was held in Rio de Janeiro, Brazil, from 13 to 22 June 2012.

The preparations for Rio+20 highlighted "seven areas that need priority attention: sustainable urban areas, food security and sustainable agricultural reserves, water, oceans, creating jobs and decrease unemployment, renewable energy and disaster readiness" (United Nations, 2012).

The conference outcome document "The Future We Want" underlined sustainable development within every theme by creating sustainable poverty eradication objectives, agriculture, transport, urbanisation, health, and promoting full and productive employment.

18 *Legal and political dimensions*

The 2030 Agenda

As the MDGs era came to an end, a meeting was held at the United Nations headquarters in September 2016 and launched the "2030 Agenda" for Sustainable Development. The new agenda called on countries to begin efforts to achieve 17 Sustainable Development Goals (SDGs) over the next 15 years (UN, 2015).

"The seventeen Sustainable Development Goals are our shared vision of humanity and a social contract between the world's leaders and the people," said UN Secretary-General Ban Ki-moon. "They are a to-do list for people and planet, and a blueprint for success" (*United Nations*, *2015a)*.

The 17 Sustainable Development Goals recognised creating jobs and economic growth through industrialisation and agriculture, ending poverty and sustaining the environment must go hand-in-hand. It addressed a wide range of basic social needs that preserve human dignity, including education, healthcare, social protection for vulnerable groups, and creating job opportunities, in addition to tackling climate change and environmental protection (United Nations, 2015a).

"Paris Agreement", 2015

The "Paris Agreement" is an agreement adopted by consensus on 12 December 2015, in Paris, France, to deal with the same framework of UNFCCC. It is a separate agreement not related to the "Kyoto Protocol", even though it reduces greenhouse gas emissions and mitigates global warming.

The "Paris Agreement" entered into force on 4 November 2016. Its central aim is to "strengthen the global response to the threat of climate change by maintaining a global temperature rise this century well below 2 degrees Celsius above pre-industrial levels and pursuing efforts to limit the temperature increase even further to 1.5 degrees Celsius" (United Nations Climate Change, 2015 b). (added b here)

Principles of international environmental law

From the large body of international treaty law and state practice, it is possible to determine some generally accepted principles. In this section, we will discuss the seven principles of IEL.

A sovereign shall make no harm

This principle is driven from states' sovereignty over natural resources and the prohibition to cause trans-boundary environmental harm. It is reflected in "Principle 21" of the "Stockholm Declaration" and "Principle 2" of the "Rio Declaration".

The duty to prevent

This duty requires the prevention of damage and harm to the environment in the states' boundaries and other territories or persons. States and other actors should adopt policies that reduce, limit, or control activities that might cause or risk such damage (Goba, 2004).

This duty adds to the obligations of "Principle 21/Principle 2" and can be regarded as a goal by itself. However, under this preventive principle lies another principle; "a state may be under an 'obligation' to prevent transboundary harm and damage to the environment within its jurisdiction" (Singh, 1986). The same principle was concluded by the court in the "Trail Smelter Case" mentioned earlier.

The principle of cooperation

This principle has been endorsed in "Principle 24" of the "Stockholm Declaration"/and "Principle 27" of the "Rio Declaration". It reinforces political commitment to international cooperation to protect the environment.

The principle of sustainable development

This principle emphasises fair use of natural resources to preserve present and future generations' rights in such resources and the commitment to integrate environmental concerns into trade, consumption, and economic development.

Legal elements related to sustainable development usually comprise several principles, including

> the need to preserve and sustain the use of natural resources taking into consideration the rights and the benefit of future generations (intergenerational equity), equity in use (intra-generational equity), the appropriate use of resources in a conscious manner (sustainable use), and finally, the inclusion of environmental concerns into economic, growth and development plans (integration).
> (Mauerhofer, 2016)

The precautionary principle

Precautions must be taken before causing damage or threatening the environment. This principle's meaning, application, and effect are controversial, as it aims to guide the development and application of IEL, especially where enough scientific data is lacking. Environmental scientists aim to study the benefits and risks of decisions on the environment and inform decision-makers. The precautionary principle focuses on finding the least harmful alternative when environmental risks are posed.

Several international treaties have adopted the precautionary principle. It is echoed in "Principle 15" of the "Rio Declaration", which stipulates that "in cases of serious threats or irreversible damage, states shall not claim lack of full scientific certainty to postpone or never taking cost-effective measures to prevent environmental degradation" (United Nations, 1992).

The "polluter pays" principle

This principle indicates that the state bears the costs of its pollution. It aims to ensure that the environmental costs are reflected in the eventual market price for goods and services.

Although many regional agreements are adopting this principle in recent years, it has not grasped as much attention and acceptance as other principles like the precautionary principle. It remains controversial in the compromise language of "Principle 16" of the "Rio Declaration", which emphasises that "the polluter should, in principle, bear the costs of pollution, with due regard to the public interests and, without distorting international trade and investment" (United Nations, 1992).

The pragmatic language used in this text limits the states' responsibilities. It seeks to ensure payment at the local level rather than the international level. However, non-polluter states, sometimes, give away their "quotas" of "allowed pollution" to other polluting states in exchange of political support/leverage.

The principle of common but differentiated responsibility

It derives from "Principle 7" of the "Rio Declaration" that ensures applying equitable rules in international law and acknowledging that the developing countries have exceptional needs to implement rules of IEL.

Weaknesses of the existing environmental law

Some of the international environmental treaty system features may weaken it, making it a less powerful law enforcement tool. This section will discuss those characteristics and their effects on the application of IEL.

It is soft law

IEL is considered a soft law, which means it is not directly enforceable by national or international bodies. Soft laws are used to encourage states to incorporate international principles and norms into their national laws; however, most IEL consists of general principles and lacks specific, court-enforceable clauses.

The "softness" of international laws originates from sovereignty concerns; they are constructed in manners that avoid limiting a state's control over its land or people.

Many international agreements include reservations made by individual states to preserve their right to decline to apply certain parts of the agreement. Exercising this right reduces the overall effectiveness of many international agreements.

While some environmental agreements like the "Montreal Protocol" have established institutions that can impose direct sanctions, others, like the "International Convention for the Regulation of Whaling", allow member states to impose trade sanctions against the violators. However, imposing such sanctions is problematic as there is no formal international body responsible for enforcing IEL. The task of direct enforcement ultimately rests on member states whose authorities advocate and adopt implementing policies.

Science-economy trade-offs

During the processes of creation and implementation of environmental agreements, a plethora of factors are taken into account. Nevertheless, the most influential factors are mainly science and the economy.

On the one hand, states are keen on ensuring that their economic interests are taken into consideration when developing and applying IEL. On the other hand, environmental regulations should only be applied with compelling scientific evidence to support it. Usually, states are reluctant to enter treaties establishing obligations where there is scientific uncertainty or no consensus on the existence of environmental harm.

The contemporary dispute over climate change science has brought uncertainty and has constrained legal developments. The scientific foundation of IEL is driven by the differences in perspectives between the United States and the European Union. The United States urges the reliance on "hard science" and leaves little room for uncertainty, while the EU allows decision-makers a more significant "margin of appreciation in the face of scientific uncertainty" (Trenberth, 2010).

On the other hand, environmental protection and the application of IEL is linked to economic development. While some states may choose to enforce stringent environmental standards, which might cause significant economic losses, others may exploit those conditions to relax their environmental standards and gain competitive economic advantages. Only rarely do environmental treaties provide economic compensation for the additional costs of protective measures. In such cases, the parties ensure that the treaty establishes compliance measures that prevent the competitive advantage linked to non-compliance.

Countries are inclined to accept or refuse to participate in international treaties because of their economic interests. They rarely make such decisions based on altruistic motives. When they accept taking part, they usually expect economic or political benefits in the longer run. Nevertheless, some treaties provide financing for developing countries in compensation for the costs of the application of IEL. This linkage with economic development has provided additional authority to IEL.

International environmental law challenges

In addition to the complexities and paradoxes of dealing with states' issues, and yet larger than states themselves, IEL faces a few challenges, namely, state compliance, enforcement procedures, and implementation strategies.

Compliance

Even though States are the ones signing treaties and conventions, transnational corporations usually violate international agreements.

It is almost impossible to sue a state for not enforcing the law, and only states can sue other states, a right not enjoyed by either individuals or non-governmental organisations. This has several ramifications on compliance with international agreements.

First, it means that the environmental damage must be so significant that the state notices it.

Second, the damage must be directly affecting its own state.

Third, the damage must be linked to the state being sued, which is difficult to demonstrate in environmental issues.

Moreover, given the vast imbalance of power between states and that no one state can be compliant with all international agreements at any moment in time, suing other states seems to be unlikely since it may expose the plaintiff state to retaliation.

Compliance in international law is an inherently difficult task. Many treaties only provide a framework for action, and even those who provide enforcement measures and forums for litigation are mostly unenforceable. No treaty or convention can force actions onto other states that refuse to comply. One can impose sanctions or order damages, restrict trade, or declare non-compliance. Nevertheless, beyond that, no one can coerce a state into compliance.

Enforcement

Over the last few decades, international agreements and treaties have become more common. However, few international courts or tribunals seem willing to take environmental protection matters into their hands. Beyond human rights, non-state actors are unlikely to be able to influence environmental protection laws largely.

Environmental organisations have continually been involved in monitoring and have sought to pressure governments into compliance with international environmental laws and standards. Although their actions have yielded significant influence in the realm of environmental diplomacy and treaty development, their effects on enforcement remain limited.

States have refrained from transferring too much enforcement power to international organisations in order to protect their sovereignty. As a result, international organisations have limited roles. "Agenda 21" and the "Rio Declaration", UNCED allowed a more significant enforcement part for international organisations to enforce laws and obligations before national and local courts.

Implementation

Although international environmental laws deal with shared environment and issues beyond national boundaries, many states' obligations must be enforced within those national borders. Domestic implementation remains the key to achieving environmental goals and causing meaningful impact.

In the face of economic dissuasion, ineffective non-governmental influence, and lack of support, more outstanding efforts must be made to persuade states to implement international law at the national level. These efforts require exploring the reasons behind inadequate domestic implementation and building focus and momentum towards action to improve it.

Bibliography

Bratspies, R.M. & Miller, R.A., 2008. Transboundary Harm in International Law: Lessons from the Trail Smelter Arbitration. *The American Journal of International Law*, 102(2), pp. 395–400.

Goba, D., 2004. Le Principe de Prevention en Droit International de l'Environnement. *Revue Ivorienne de Droit*, 36(9).

IUCN, UNEP, WWF, 2009. *Caring for the Earth: A Strategy for Sustainable Living*. New York: Earthscan.

Kanie, N., 2007. Governance with Multilateral Environmental Agreements: A Healthy or Ill-Equipped Fragmentation? In W. Hoffmann & L. Swart, eds. *Global Environmental Governance: Perspectives on the Current Debate*. New York: Center for UN, pp. 67–86.

Mauerhofer, V., 2016. *Legal Aspects of Sustainable Development*. Cham: Springer.
OHCHR, 2000. *United Nations Millennium Declaration*. [Online] Available at: https://unfccc.int/process/the-kyoto-protocol/the-doha-amendment [Accessed 4 June 2020].
Singh, N., 1986. Foreword. In R. Munro, ed. *Environmental Protection and Sustainable Development: Legal Principles and Recommendations*. Netherlands: Springer, pp. xi–xii.
Trenberth, K., 2010. More Knowledge, Less Certainty. *Nature Climate Change*, 1(1002), pp. 20–21.
UN, 2000. *Millennium Goals*. [Online] Available at: www.un.org/millenniumgoals/ [Accessed 3 June 2020].
UN, 2015. *Transforming Our World: The 2030 Agenda for Sustainable Development*. New York: United Nations.
UNCED, 1992. *Agenda 21*. [Online] Available at: https://sustainabledevelopment.un.org/index.php?page=view&nr=23&type=400&menu=35 [Accessed 3 June 2020].
UNEP, 2012. *The Emissions Gap Report 2012*. Nairobi: United Nations Environment Programme.
UNFCC, 2020. *The Doha Amendment*. [Online] Available at: https://unfccc.int/process/the-kyoto-protocol/the-doha-amendment [Accessed 3 March 2021].
United Nations Climate Change, 2015. *The Web Page*. [Online] Available at: https://unfccc.int/process-and-meetings/the-paris-agreement/the-paris-agreement [Accessed 5 June 2020].
United Nations, 1972. *United Nations Conference on the Human Environment, Stockholm*. Stockholm: United Nations.
United Nations, 1992. *Report of the UN Conference on Environment and Development. CONF.151/26/Rev.1*. Vols. I–III. Rio de Janeiro: United Nations.
United Nations, 2004. *Johannesburg Declaration on Sustainable Development – From Our Origins to the Future*. [Online] Available at: www.un.org/esa/sustdev/documents/WSSD_POI_PD/English/POI_PD.htm#1/ [Accessed 4 June 2020].
United Nations, 2007. *Enable FAQ*. [Online] Available at: www.un.org/esa/socdev/enable/convinfofaq.htm [Accessed 22 May 2020].
United Nations, 2011. *Review of Implementation of the Rio Principles*. New York: United Nations.
United Nations, 2012. *About the Rio+20 Conference*. [Online] at: www.un.org/esa/sustdev/documents/WSSD_POI_PD/English/POI_PD.htm#1/ [Accessed 4 June 2020].
United Nations, 2015a. *17 Goals to Transform our World*. [Online] at: www.un.org/sustainabledevelopment/ [Accessed 5 June 2020].
United Nations, 2015b. *Paris Agreement*. New York: United Nations.
United Nations, 2015c. *The Millennium Development Goals Report, 2015*. New York: United Nations.
World Commission on Environment and Development, 1987. *Report of the World Commission on Environment and Development: Our Common Future*. London: Oxford University Press.

3 Environmental issues at international and regional levels
Informal diplomacy

An ENGO (environmental non-governmental organisation) is an NGO in the field of the environment. They operate locally and internationally, and play an essential role in addressing different environmental issues in the contemporary world. One of the most distinguishing features of environmental NGOs from environmental movements is that environmental NGOs have organisational charters that set out rules for distributing power among the people who are part of them. These organisations exist around the world and, since the 1980s, they have increasingly influenced environmental policy and discourse globally.

Usually, NGOs are independent of any government institutions, but many receive EU funds to carry out their actions in the European Union. Through programmes such as LIFE, a financing instrument for the environment and climate action created in 1992, the EU finances organisations that work within this scope. For the 2014–2020 funding period, the programme had a budget of 3.4 billion euros.

This may raise some questions about the level of independence and legitimacy of these organisations. As Transparency International points out, NGO status risks become a mere vehicle used by special interest groups to circumvent control mechanisms. This is already happening with Astroturf, which Laurens defines as the "process by which firms create mobilisations that take the form of an NGO, resemble an NGO but whose existence is, in fact, provided by private funds, for commercial purposes"(Laurens,2015).

The organisations' widespread influence highlights the importance of their advocacy plans and role in the adoption and implementation of environmental plans.

In this chapter, we study the ways, means, and challenges ENGOs face at the environmental field, we use the European "Green Deal" as a case study.

A brief history of European environmental law

Environmental policy is one of the first areas of EU intervention. It ranks third among common policies in 2015 in terms of the number of laws. While estimates of the national/European law ratio differ from year to year and country to country, this is undoubtedly one of the most Europeanised policies. It is recognised as the most comprehensive environmental legislation in the world, covering its usual areas: quality of water, air, energy, industrial products, consumer information, noise, and waste. The recognition of the environment by European treaties, first in 1986, has steadily increased since then.

In 2019 in her article about the role of lobbies in the making of environmental standards, Nathalie Berny made this observation: environmental law is now carried out at the European level. However, this pre-eminence of the EU in the environmental field has not always existed, and it has been achieved gradually, through several key stages:

1986: The Single European Act introduced a specific competence of the EU on the subject of the environment since it can be read that "The requirements in terms of environmental protection are a component of the other policies of the community".

1992: The Maastricht Treaty made the environment a European policy with the latter's entry into the field of co-decision.

1997: The Amsterdam Treaty recognised the principle of sustainable development "which meets present needs without compromising the ability of future generations to meet theirs".

2009: The Treaty of Lisbon adds the "promotion, at the international level, of measures intended to deal with regional or planetary environmental problems, and in particular the fight against climate change".

The European "Green Deal" is a set of political initiatives from the European Commission whose main objective is to make Europe climate neutral by 2050. A plan subject to an impact assessment will also be presented to increase the objective of reducing the EU's greenhouse gas emissions for 2030 to at least 50% and towards 55% compared to 1990 levels. This plan provides for reviewing each existing law based on its merits on the climate plan and introducing new legislation on the circular economy, building renovation, biodiversity, agriculture, and innovation.

Specific provisions of this plan are still under constant renegotiation between the various groups in Parliament and the Commission and the interest groups.

This is how the Union gradually emerged as the leading legislator in terms of environmental policy. This is primarily explained by the single market, making it challenging to take environmental measures at the national level since these could cause decreased competitiveness for the country in question and, therefore, a distortion of competition between the member states. This is why the defence of the environmental cause is mainly done in Brussels.

The EU and interest groups: relationship wanted, assumed, negotiated

Interest groups can, as Offerlé explains, "be seen as instruments of expression of the general will or as parasitic bodies tending to monopolise the production and control of political goods".

Within the framework of this study, we use this definition: "representative (re) groups, lasting or occasional, that their spokespersons make act to promote, primarily or incidentally, the defense of social interests, of whatever nature".

Interest groups are catalysts for collective action because they articulate social expectations and actively intervene to ensure that they are taken into consideration by the public authorities. In doing so, they constitute full-fledged players in the political system and help shape effective operation rules.

The term "advocacy" is also often associated with "interest groups" and "lobbying". In general, the term "lobbying" is considered to be used to describe activities which attempt to influence legislation for the benefit of personal or private interests; "advocacy" would describe the representation of interests for the benefit of a third party or an external group and, technically, does not focus solely on the legislative aspect. In the Brussels context of the EU, we see that all interest groups are treated in the same way and considered to be carrying out lobbying activities, be private, public, or non-governmental bodies.

One of the lobbying challenges is its very strong interweaving with the political world, as Courty points out. In the Brussels context, Michel highlights the system of revolving doors: the passage of lobbyists from the public sphere to the private sphere and vice versa; this is what she calls the circular dimension of careers. Companies recruit former employees of ministerial offices or parliamentary assistants: a kind of self-esteem is formed where the border between public/private is relatively absent. Indeed, as Courty notes, these are complex and ambiguous relationships

> between political professionals who stress that they need these products in order to know, see, understand the state of society and of representatives. interests which underline that they must also produce these

figures to reassure their constituents by thus demonstrating that they are working effectively and efficiently for them.

In this sense, we note that the borders of the political field in Bourdieu's sense are here porous, and the political and social world is intertwined. In the European political field, there are therefore civil servants and politicians but also all the other actors who participate in it: representatives of interest, representatives of causes, commissioners, bosses, unions. These borders must therefore be widened, and the political field thus becomes what Georgakakis calls the "field of Eurocracy", space to which "the political and administrative elites of the member states and many European social and economic groups delegate part of their political, social and economic mission. . . . It is like the concrete operator" (Parthenay, 2013).

Interest groups within the EU

In the context of the European Union, interest groups are a central part of the political process; as Michel asserts, the impact of these groups' activities in the process of integration and construction of the Union is undeniable (Michel, 2013).

For European institutions, interest groups are the embodiment of the people and civil society. In this sense, they are associated with decision-making processes, and their perception is far from the vision of influence and corruption that they may have elsewhere. In this context, the European Union tries to adopt measures to ensure transparent, democratic, and honest lobbying, to fill the democratic deficit and prevent corruption situations. Therefore, the entire European political system is organised on a permanent consultation between officials, commissioners, and representatives of interests. The European institutions operate transparently as a permanent game of information and expertise exchange with other actors, making politics the product of permanent interaction between those with expertise and political actors.

Since the Treaty of Rome, interest groups have been recognised as full-fledged players in European integration, and since the 1960s they have been listed. At that time, interest groups were still not powerful actors on the European political level, but since the 1990s, the European institutions will be primarily invested by these groups (Aldrin, 2013).

In 2011, the Commission created a transparency register that lists all interest groups active with the institutions, without distinguishing between public and private interest groups. Since 2014, only interest representatives registered in this transparency register, now more than 12,000, can officially meet with the auditors, members of their cabinets, and general managers (Transparency Register, 2021). This has become a necessary passage point to access European decision-makers.

In the context of the EU, lobbying is therefore seen as "a legitimate activity within a democratic system, whether carried out by citizens or businesses, civil society organisations and other groups of citizens' interests or by companies working on behalf of third parties"(Coen, 1998). These groups provide very detailed information for creating public policies and strengthening the democratic functioning of the EU by conferring a kind of legitimisation from below.

The advocacy of environmental NGOs, lobbying unlike any other

Environmental issues can and do take on the character of bottom-up politics, yet parliamentary activism in environmental arenas reflects the widespread status of high politics issues (Wurzel & Connelly, 2010). In turn, this high general political status means that environmental NGOs' interests have been able to influence European public affairs and have themselves contributed to this degree of politicisation. Such patterns are somewhat less evident in consumer affairs and social affairs, although they are not absent at all. Nevertheless, how have environmental NGOs been able to exert this pressure to effect this change in policies from the bottom up?

Burson-Marstellar's "Guide to Effective Lobbying of the European Parliament" stated that MEPs considered environmental non-governmental organisations to be the most effective at lobbying. Almost one in four MEPs – 24% – cited environmental NGOs when asked which sectors they believe are most effective at lobbying. With their mass of members and the skills acquired by their European offices, environmental organisations "allow them to combine institutional politics with the traditional activism of the social movement" (Burson-Marsteller Report, 2021).

The advocacy of environmental NGOs in the social world of the EU is a product of the electoral failures of the 1990s and 2005. After the electoral trials of the 1990s and the increase in Eurosceptic votes, the EU begins to experiment with new principles integration and legitimation (Aldrin & Hube, 2016).

In other words, the notion of participation has undergone a radical change. The EU has established and supervised representations of civil society and the market. Through this framework, the EU created a mediation body with European civil society, the EESC in 1999. The EESC is defined as the mediation body between citizens and public authorities. The EU has broadened the scope of participation and the modalities of democracy after discovering evidence of corruption between EU officials and expert groups (Weisbein, 2003). The changing political arena of the EU helps us observe the emergence of distinct

European lobbying strategies and complex advocacy coalitions which take advantage of new opportunity structures (MacMullen, 1999).

Relations between parliament and "weaker" civic interest groups can be seen as what some European academics have called "advocacy coalitions". These groups' primary strategy was to pressure the Commission and the Council as final objectives through parliament. This had a considerable impact on the inter-institutional balance. Today, the Commission and the Parliament are not always allies representing the European interest, but find themselves in competition for legitimacy.

Still present during the formation of the Community and the European Union, corporate political activity exploded in the 1990s, building on the access offered by the single market programme and the creeping regulatory powers of the EU. In response to this increasingly crowded and competitive lobbying environment, corporate interests have developed new direct lobbying strategies, collective action agreements, complex political advocacy alliances, and tailored national interest models (Morgera, 2012).

Civil society: a democratic ideal built for and by the European institutions

One of the best references on European civil society is P. Aldrin book entitled "The "European civil society", between democratic ideal and political contingencies". He tells that Europe was first of all made up of the economic actors who participated from the start in its creation. Construction with the Consultative Committee established by the CECA brings together professionals in the coal and steel sectors. Europe, therefore, began from its origins to work with economic organisations and lobbies. Nevertheless, in the 1990s, criticism of the influence of these private interest groups not representing citizens began to mount. It was during this period that the concept of "European civil society" was born in academia (Aldrin, 2013).

According to Julien Weisbein, it designates

> rather metaphorically, among some social science researchers, the growing aggregation of national societies in an increasingly decompartmentalised market where, on a horizontal basis, the mobility of people, goods, services and capital erases borders and redraws the contours of an increasingly united sociological whole, in particular through transnational links increased.
>
> (Weisben, 2003)

Therefore, this concept was born to qualify the fruit of the compartmentalisation of markets between European countries, and Weibstein tells that

Environmental issues 31

the European institutions have gradually adopted this concept throughout laws and Commission publications. In parallel with the growth of its administrative use, civil society manifested through the rise of citizen movements at the end of the 1990s.

According to Philippe Aldrin, these demonstrations accelerated the process of valuing citizen pressure groups, that is to say, the moral lobbying of transnational humanitarian, citizen, and ecological NGOs which are multiplying, in a context of weakening of the Europe which results in abstention from the European elections and the dropping of opinions favourable to integration in the Eurobarometer (Aldrin, 2013). This, according to Aldrin and Hubé, attests to "the failure of the path chosen so far to develop European democracy". It was then from 2001 that the process of valuing European civil society was formalised, with the publication of the "White Paper on European governance" which defended participation as one of the main principles of "more democratic" governance (Aldrin & Hubé, 2016"a").

As Hélène Michel writes, this increase is part of a "logic of re-legitimising EU institutions among citizens who are increasingly suspicious of and not interested in European politics" (Michel, 2007). However, although this new mode of governance was born out of institutions to strengthen their legitimacy, Aldrin stresses that it is a concept that is debated within these. Indeed, the author underlines how much the strengthening of civil society in European governance leads to reluctance and opposition from the European Parliament, which itself elected by universal suffrage claims to be the sole representative of society (Aldrin, 2013).

The use of European civil society by the Commission was therefore made to fill the democratic deficit that the EU was facing, despite the European Parliament's reluctance, which thus found itself competing for democratic legitimacy by the Commission.

Environmental advocacy at international and regional levels: successes and failures

The first part of this section will present the finding results of a comparative case study, between two active NGOs in Brussels: the European Environmental Bureau (EEB) and Greenpeace European Unit. The second will highlight the challenges that lead to the failure of United Nations Sustainable Development Solutions Network (UNSDSN).

European Environmental Bureau

The EEB is an organisation that presents itself as the largest network of environmental organisations in Europe, bringing together more than 160 member organisations in more than 35 countries. The EEB claims to represent more than 30 million individual members (EEB, 2021).

Founded in Brussels in 1974, this federation of environmental organisations is part of the GREEN 10, a coalition of the ten largest environmental NGOs active at European level.

The BEE advocates for sustainable development, environmental justice, global equity, transparency, and participatory democracy. The values displayed by the organisation are democracy, fairness, respect, integrity, and sustainability. Its main activities are described as follows: agenda-setting, monitoring, expertise, and influence on how the EU deals with these issues. Its main activity is the European Union and its decision-making processes.

BEE's influencing work on the energy decarbonisation strategy within Green Deal

The advocacy work carried out by the EEB to defend decarbonisation within the European Green Deal did not begin once it was presented to the general public. Indeed, we can see in the 2019 report published by the BEE that it acted throughout the electoral and political process which led to the publication of the Green Deal, with actions in four stages:

Before the European elections

- A manifesto written alongside their Green10 partners.
- An internet page gathering resources and documents for voters and candidates.

After the elections

- A letter sent to all newly elected deputies.
- An open letter signed by more than 150 NGOs addressed to European leaders so that sustainable development is placed at the heart of the 2019–2024 strategic agenda.

Before Ms Van Der Leyen presidency

Before electing Van Der Leyen as President of the Commission by the European Parliament, media pressured for the "green wave" with the slogan "From Green Wave to Green New Deal".

Van der Leyen era and Green Deal

With the election of Ms Van der Leyen and the announcement of the European Green Deal, progress has been made through:

- The influence on the content and ambition of the programme.
- The publication of a detailed report listing the Green Deal's priorities, with carbon neutrality as the number one priority.

The director of European policies, Patrick ten Brick, congratulated himself by affirming that Mrs Van der Leyen made the right choice by placing the European Green Deal at the forefront of her political agenda, which signals the victory of the agenda of environmental organisations.

In addition to the public lobbying strategy with open and manifest letters, the BEE monitored the Green Deal's various issues, including decarbonisation.

Going back to the chronology leading up to the elections, we can see how much the EEB was attached to influencing the agenda of European policies throughout the campaign and even today in the application of the European Green Deal. While during the election campaign its work consisted of public appeals, manifestos, and open letters, we can now see that the office is more concerned with publishing reports and following up on the Green Deal's political promises, in particular, to defend decarbonisation.

Greenpeace

Presentation of Greenpeace European Unit

Greenpeace's European unit is part of the international network of Greenpeace, active in more than 55 countries around the world. As stated on their official website, based in Brussels, the Greenpeace EU team monitors and analyses EU institutions' work, exposes flawed policies and laws, and calls on decision-makers to put in place solutions adapted to people and the planet.

As they describe it, their goal is to ensure the Earth's ability to nurture life in all its diversity. In this sense, their main actions are the protection of biodiversity in all its forms, prevention of pollution, and misuse of oceans, land, air, and freshwater, the end of all nuclear threats and the promotion of peace, global disarmament, and non-violence.

They state their core values as personal responsibility and non-violence, independence, has no permanent friends or enemies, and promote solutions.

The influence of Greenpeace on the energy decarbonisation strategy within Green Deal

As part of the energy decarbonisation strategy enshrined in the Green Deal, Greenpeace has participated in its promotion differently.

Before the Green Deal was approved, Greenpeace, along with two other organisations, orchestrated a street protest to call for political action on climate change. The action aimed to put pressure on energy and environment ministers who were to meet in Brussels to discuss whether to support a plan to fully decarbonise the EU by 2050.

Actions based on scandalisation to show the springs of injustice, of the betrayal of elites, and of the absurd consequences of a public decision.

Greenpeace published research last September to serve as a roadmap for European decision-makers to decarbonise the transport sector by 2040, by making it operational using renewable energies, without resorting to biofuels. Consulting firms was Climate and New Climate Institute.

Greenpeace also collaborated in the publication of a report last October entitled "Decarbonizing Is Easy: Beyond Market Neutrality in the ECB's Corporate QE" which aims to reveal how the policy of "market neutrality" proclaimed by the ECB promotes the buying of products. Corporate bonds of the bank in favour of carbon-intensive industries. On the same line, Greenpeace denounced last month, during a press briefing, the pressure exerted by the gas industry on the EU to adopt criteria for classifying gas as a green fuel, through an open letter signed by the leading industrial groups in the sector (GreenPeace, 2021);

United Nations Sustainable Development Solutions Network (UNSDSN): a failed strategy

United Nations Sustainable Development Solutions Network (SDSN) is an organisation organised by national and regional networks to interact with institutions in their respective countries.

SDSN was established in 2012, at the request of UN Secretary-General Ban Ki-moon, to mobilise global scientific and technological expertise to promote practical problem-solving solutions for sustainable development. It was registered in the State of Delaware, the United States, to "operate exclusively for charitable, religious, scientific and educational purposes". It has two offices: in Paris and New York (Sustainable Development Solutions Network, 2021).

Unlike EEB and Greenpeace, which accept financial contributions from their members, the SDSN works under grants usually provided by international organisations, civil society, academia, and the private sector.

However, their audit reports did not specify the types of grants received or from what source exactly. Therefore, private sector funding could lead us to question the extent to which this association can be considered an "Astroturf" (Laurens, 2015).

The organisation's mission is to "support the implementation of the SDGs at local, national and global scales". In their respective countries and regions, the networks of universities, research centres and other knowledge institutions of SDSN translate the latest sustainable development skills into action by "Localise and mobilise support for the SDGs, Promote high-quality education and research collaboration; Verification and launch of solution initiatives"(Le Naëlou, 2004).

SDSN has contributed to European Policy Network through its participation in the research project "The World in 2050" (TWI2050). In this fixing the business of food, how to align the agro-food sector with the SDGs' Publication. As a result, they have also mobilised their deep core beliefs by integrating them into EU-funded projects that incorporate their policy core beliefs (Sustainable Development Solutions Network, 2021).

In other words, their professionalisation and understanding of European policies are essential because European public policies are based on these subsystems, which are very stable and very consolidated accepting little space for other conceptions of politics. Therefore, it is Andrija Eric, Network Manager of SDSN Paris, who confirms that:

> However, the needs in terms of integrating the SDGs into the daily lives of member countries also require action at European level. Within the framework of the European Semester, for example, which is organised in exchanges between the European Commission and the member countries, organisations like SDSN must act on both levels. By acting at European level, we seek to defend the place of the SDGs in the general strategy and in European priorities. By acting at the national level, our networks seek to ensure the concrete integration of the SDGs into national policies.

In their scientific neutrality in their participation in the projects already mentioned, Eric adds that "By keeping our independence vis-à-vis the political sphere in the drafting of our reports, we thus maintain a certain neutrality, but also a degree of realism and honesty which brings us credibility in the advice given" (Andrija, 2020).

As part of its advocacy work on the Green Deal, the SDSN has contributed to the adoption of this framework by accessing the register of expert groups. SDSN was also part of the experts of the formal and informal group. Members of the SDSN role have provided advice to the Commission on the research portfolio and opened a dialogue with the member states, the European Parliament, and stakeholders.

Another lobbying tool mobilised by SDSN is the organisation of events. Organising events "we also seek to facilitate exchanges between scientists and other stakeholders without taking part in the political debates per se" (Andrija, 2020).

While the EEB and the European unit of Greenpeace have direct offices in Brussels and both are registered in the European transparency register in order to be able to meet the members of the Commission, UNSDSN is headquartered in Paris and is not on the register as such. However, SDSN has been a member of several expert groups with the European Union (four groups mention it) and has published numerous reports and documents which have influenced European environmental policy.

Greenpeace is one example of an international organisation whose office in Brussels carries out some institutional activities and organises demonstrations, staging in public space and numerous press releases. However, the SDSN does not carry out lobbying activity per se. However, its active participation in international expertise on environmental issues is an indirect means of defending Brussels' environmental cause.

Conclusion

Cases showed that there are challenges defending the environmental cause in Brussels. Indeed, it is understandable that the EU took part in the constitution and the political participation of these organisations to fill the democratic deficit it faced. The institutionalisation of these environmental organisations has led them to adopt the codes and behaviours of economic lobbying that have been present with the EU since the birth of the latter. However, the maintenance of social and media pressure for the environmental cause in Europe shows that citizens themselves influence environmental policies and NGOs: professionalisation has, therefore, not hampered the means of influence specific to society: European civil. While appropriating the classic tools of lobbying, environmental NGOs rely on civic events and actions for the climate throughout Europe through strong institutionalisation. The comparative case study confirms the diversity of the means of action used for environmental advocacy in Europe and its complementarity in influencing the European institution. Besides, in implementing a European programme such as the Green Deal, environmental advocacy has been carried out throughout the process with tools of expertise, communication, and media pressure used from the outset: European elections, then in the pre-cooking of the green pact, and finally in its concrete application. The reports of the SDSN, the letters in manifestos of the BEE, and the actions organised by Greenpeace were all able to contribute to the setting on the agenda of the environmental cause, and then to its implementation in accordance with the wishes of the civil society and the experts.

Environmental advocacy in Brussels presents a hybrid form of lobbying which is at the same time citizen, media, political, and expert.

Environmental NGOs adopt both the classic lobbying tools through meetings with leaders and the publication of expert reports, and tools from modern collective action directories with climate strikes, but also happening or demonstrations. Through these actions, NGOs pose as representatives of civil society, working with or against institutions to participate in policy development or denounce their environmental inaction. However, the importance of these organisations' expert reports shows another strategy of influence, which illustrates the theory of domination by virtue of Weber's knowledge, specific to our rational-legal societies: indeed, NGOs are gaining in influence. Through their expertise, which provides real support for the implementation of European environmental policies. Bourdieu's field theory also allows us to understand both the influence of the SDSN, however outside the European world, and the essential professionalisation of NGOs in European policies and legislation. Indeed, the SDSN expert groups, which do not operate in Brussels as such, are located in a neutral place described by Bourdieu as the working link between the academic field and power. On the contrary, to be an actor in the influence game within European institutions such as Greenpeace and even more the BEE, knowledge of European legislation, networks, and methods used by institutions that environmental NGOs can be situated and act directly with institutions. This knowledge of the European world, which has its functioning, is essential to influence political processes.

We, therefore, clearly understand the various advocacy tools and strategies of environmental NGOs. Their number and diversity of actors make it possible to maintain a local anchoring close to citizens and participate in the development of policies with the Commission. Also, one can question more broadly about the role of politics and ideological debate in shaping EU public policies. Indeed, by setting up working groups and experts directly with civil society and NGOs, the Commission doubles the European Parliament in its role of representing the people and does not raise the question of the debate of ideas to which it prefers the construction of the general interest through compromise.

Bibliography

About EEB - EEB - The European Environmental Bureau (no date). Available at: https://eeb.org/homepage/about/ (Accessed: 22 April 2021).

Aldrin, P., 2013. La 'société civile européenne', entre idéal démocratique et contingences politiques: De Maastricht à Lisbonne, les mises à l'agenda parlementaire de l'ouverture aux lobbys et à la société civil. Larcier. *Le Parlement européen après Lisbonne, Larcier.* (Dossiers), pp. 183–226.

Aldrin, P. & Hubé, N., 2016a. *L'État participatif.* Paris: Presses de Sciences Po.

Aldrin, P. & Hube, N., 2016b. L'Union européenne, une démocratie destakeholders. *Gouvernement & action publique*, 2(2), p. 125. https://doi.org/10.3917/gap.162.0125.

Erac, A. (2020) 'Interview with SDSN Network Manager Paris'.

Berkhout, J., 2016. Lobbying in the European Union: Interest Groups, Lobbying Coalitions and Policy Change. *Public administration (London)*, 94(1), pp. 278–280. https://doi.org/10.1111/padm.12231.

Berny, N., 2008. Le lobbying des ONG internationales d'environnement à Bruxelles. *Revue française de science politique*, 58(1), pp. 97–121. https://doi.org/10.3917/rfsp.581.0097.

Berny, N., 2014. Les entrepreneurs de coalition d'ONG à Bruxelles. Une approche diachronique des processus de mobilisation de ressources. *Gouvernement & action publique*, (1), pp. 75–105. https://doi.org/10.3917/gap.141.0075.

Betsill, M.M. & Corell, E., 2001. NGO Influence in International Environmental Negotiations: A Framework for Analysis. *Global Environmental Politics*, 1(4), pp. 65–85. https://doi.org/10.1162/152638001317146372.

Burson-Marsteller Report: A Guide to Effective Lobbying of the European Commission, Issuu, 2021. Available at: https://issuu.com/burson-marsteller-emea/docs/guideeurcom (Accessed: 22 April 2021).

Chapoulie, J.-M., 1973. Sur l'analyse sociologique des groupes professionnels. *Revue française de sociologie*, 14(1), pp. 86–114. https://doi.org/10.2307/3320324.

Coen, D., 1998. The European Business Interest and the Nation State: Large-firm Lobbying in the European Union and Member States. *Journal of Public Policy*, 18(1), pp. 75–100. https://doi.org/10.1017/S0143814X9800004X.

Courty, G., 2011. La sociologie politique des groupes d'intérêt et la construction européenne. *Fare. Frontières, Acteurs et représentations de l'Europe*, (1), pp. 93–111.

Donoghue, J.E., 1994. *The International Politics of the Environment.* Edited by Andrew Hurrell and Benedict Kingsbury. Oxford and New York: Oxford University Press, 1992, pp. xiv, 469.

Dvořáková, D. & Petrůj, M., 2013. Lobbying in the European Union – Regulation and Public Sector Economics Perspective. *Acta UniversitatisAgriculturae et SilviculturaeMendelianaeBrunensis*, 61(2), pp. 327–333. https://doi.org/10.11118/actaun201361020327.

Erika, A., 2020. Interview avec SDSN Network Manager Paris.

Folmer, H. & Jeppesen, T., 2003. Environmental policy in the European Union: Community Competence vs Member State Competence. *Tijdschrift Voor Economische Sociale Geografie*, 94(4), pp. 510–515. https://doi.org/10.1111/1467-9663.00277.

Greenpeace European Unit (2021). Available at: https://www.greenpeace.org/eu-unit/ (Accessed: 22 April 2021).

Hamidi, C., 2012. De quoi un cas est-il le cas ? Penser les cas limites. *Politix*, (100), pp. 85–98. https://doi.org/10.3917/pox.100.0085.

Laurens, S., 2015. Astroturfs et ONG de consommateurs téléguidées à Bruxelles. Quand le business se crée une légitimité "par en bas". *Critique internationale (Paris. 1998)*, 67(2), pp. 83–99. https://doi.org/10.3917/crii.067.0083.

Le Naëlou, A., 2004. Pour comprendre la professionnalisation dans les ONG: quelques apports d'une sociologie des professions. *Revue Tiers monde*, 45(180), pp. 773–798. https://doi.org/10.3406/tiers.2004.5528.

Michel, H., 2007. La "société civile" dans la "gouvernance européenne". *Actes de la recherche en sciences sociales*, 166–167(1), p. 30. https://doi.org/10.3917/arss.166.0031.

Michel, H., 2013. Businesseurope au-delà du "lobbying": le travail d'intégration européenne d'une organisation patronale. *Critique internationale (Paris. 1998)*, 59(2), pp. 133–155. https://doi.org/10.3917/crii.059.0133.

Morgera, E., 2012. *The External Environmental Policy of the European Union*. Cambridge: Cambridge University Press.

Parthenay, K., 2013. Le champ de l'Eurocratie. Une sociologie politique du personnel de l'UE. (Études politiques). *Revue française de science politique*, 63(1), pp. 118–119.

Sustainable Development Solutions Network (2021). Available at: https://www.unsdsn.org/ (Accessed: 22 April 2021).

Transparency register (2021) *European Commission - European Commission*. Available at: https://ec.europa.eu/info/about-european-commission/service-standards-and-principles/transparency/transparency-register_en (Accessed: 22 April 2021).

Weible, C.M. et al., 2011. A Quarter Century of the Advocacy Coalition Framework: An Introduction to the Special Issue. *Policy studies journal*, 39(3), pp. 349–360. https://doi.org/10.1111/j.1541-0072.2011.00412.x.

Weisbein, J., 2003. Sociogenèse de la "société civile européenne". *Raisons politiques : études de pensée politique*, 10(2), p. 125. https://doi.org/10.3917/rai.010.0125.

Wurzel, R. & Connelly, J., 2010. *The European Union As a Leader in International Climate Change Politics*. Taylor & Francis Group.

4 Towards a more effective environmental governance

Environmental governance: a working definition

Like many other similar notions in international law, there is no clear accepted definition for the term "governance", which still has relative meaning, and is subject to diverse interpretations due to the interpreters' backgrounds and over time and space.

From the *environmental* perspective, governance can be defined as a full range of laws, regulations, procedures, and institutions through which political authorities control environmental actions.

The International Institute for Sustainable Development defines "environmental governance" as the "the sum of organisations, policy instruments, financing mechanisms, rules, procedures and norms that regulate the processes of global environmental protection" (International Institute for Sustainable Development, 2006).

So, International Environmental Governance consists of multilayered communications and interactions at the global, regional, and local levels, among diverse actors such as states, the private sector, and civil society.

Key principles of environmental governance

After the proliferation of knowledge on environmental issues and sustainability and the increase of environmental challenges and concerns, environmental governance surfaced as a separate field of policy and research.

The term "governance" indicates the social function of steering society towards socially or collectively desired outcomes. This social function of governance is performed by the collective efforts of the institutions forming the governance system.

For the last few decades, decision-making powers have been decentralised, shifting from governments towards local institutions and NGOs. In the environmental governance realm, this power shift intends to achieve the fundamental principles of environmental governance, and enhance accountability, accessibility, and local communities' representation.

This power shift has been carried out in several ways, and varies in levels of effectiveness. Consequently, the need to measure the effectiveness of environmental governance evolved and gave rise to the indicators of "good governance", including the evaluation of the "key principles of good governance: legitimacy, transparency, accountability, inclusivity, fairness, integration, capability and effectiveness" (Savage et al., 2020).

The environment has become part of every level of decision-making, which results from the modern understanding that cities and communities, as well as economic, social and political life, are all subsets of the environment, and all people belong to the ecosystem in which they thrive.

Environmental policy priority areas

Policies within environmental governance tend to emphasise several aspects of environmental policy. The most notable areas are the environment and quality of life, climate change, ecosystem degradation, nature and biodiversity, natural resources, and waste management. This section will discuss each of these priority areas.

The quality of life and environment

The increase in resource consumption in the last century led to a leap in economic growth, to a point where researchers tend to correlate environmental degradation to economic growth. However, not all forms of consumption and economic growth may negatively impact and harm the environment.

Economic growth may cause environmental degradation through the over-consumption of non-renewable resources, increased emissions and pollution, and the possible loss of environmental habitats.

An association has been established between three primary issues: environmental pollution, healthcare spending, and economic growth (*refer to Case Study 4.1*).

Case Study 4.1: COVID-19 pandemic and the environment: opportunities amid disasters

Tatiana Rahbany

In late 2019, cases of viral pneumonia of unknown aetiology were registered in Wuhan, Hubei province, China. The infectious agent was later identified as a new form of coronavirus. Within a few months, the virus had swept across the globe, infecting millions and killing tens of thousands. This pandemic had such long-standing effects on the world – economy, environment, health, and society – so much so that what is beyond the pandemic looks so different than what the world knew before it. It is the "new normal".

On 11 March 2020, the World Health Organization (WHO) declared the outbreak a pandemic. Governments worldwide took stringent measures to curtail the contagion, including lockdowns, to ensure physical distancing. People were ordered to work and study from home, and all retail stores were shut down except for those providing essential goods. Governments imposed curfews, most cities were barren, and many businesses had to resort to furloughs. The pandemic had threatened the lives and livelihoods of many, and everyone scrambled to adjust.

The environment's silver lining in a chaotic COVID era

Amidst this global crisis, humanity experienced an economic crisis like never before. Stocks plummeted, and millions of jobs were lost. In the United States alone, a staggering 22 million people filed for unemployment insurance during March 2020.

At that point, there was a unanimous belief that this pandemic will define the beginning of a new era; the post-COVID world will not return to "normal". That was an exciting time; redefining business as usual. The lockdown had immense, but temporary, effects on carbon emissions evident by satellite images of China's pollution, with factories shut down and many working and learning from home and not having to burn fuel to commute.

Not only has the pandemic had immediate effects on lessening pollution, but it has also given companies, governments, and individuals a chance to align pandemic response with the imperatives of health and sustainability.

The recognition of the pandemic as an opportunity for climate diplomacy stems from recognising similarities between the pandemic and climate risk. Despite the differences in the time frame of the risks, with the pandemic evolving within months and the climate change happening over decades, the similarities are uncanny.

According to Pinner et al. (2020), pandemics and climate risk both constitute physical shocks, translating into socio-economic impacts. Moreover, physical shocks require the treatment of the underlying cause. Both pandemic and climate risks are systemic, propagating swiftly across the globe. Both are unpredictable, where past occurrences are continuously changing, making future predictions difficult. Both are non-linear, are risk multipliers, and are regressive, hitting population subgroups differently. Most importantly, the pandemic has shown us our ill-preparedness for both catastrophes.

The pandemic has forced governments and corporations to take certain steps towards sustainability. The "new normal" must focus on resilience and the long-term effects of our actions. The failure to build resilient systems, infrastructures, and supply chains has proven to be very expensive, in terms of human and economic costs. Both pandemics and climate action require global coordination and cooperation, and effective social behaviour change is an excellent determinant of success (Pinner et al., 2020).

The year 2020 was anticipated to be a pivotal year for addressing climate change efforts, as the UN Secretary-General called it. Revamped plans to reduce emissions were expected to be shared by 193 countries at the UN's annual climate summit. The summit and many other climate-related conventions had to be postponed indefinitely due to the inability to gather world leaders.

The pandemic has also affected national efforts against climate change. Many countries relaxed enforcement of climate action laws, and others halted environmental programmes altogether. COVID-19 brought back climate to the pre-environmental security era. It was once again off the political agenda.

The pandemic has indeed wreaked havoc on the global community, but it also offers an opportunity to make the "new normal" greener. The lockdown has shown that many businesses can operate remotely, reducing the need for fuel. Restarting economies included stimulus packages by Australian, US, Canadian governments, to name but a few. Those could give advantage to "greener" businesses investing in cleaner energy or those promoting less waste. Similarly, financial industry bailouts could require banks to invest less in fossil fuel and more in climate change mitigation and resilience efforts.

Those pushing for the green agenda have an opportunity, but a challenging one. While the pandemic does pose immediate threats to the livelihoods and safety of many, care must be taken to keep the environmental agenda running during this critical time. Great reflection must be made by all governments post-COVID; less fuel, emissions, and environmental degradation are indeed possible.

Nevertheless, the environment is not the only aspect of human life that the pandemic affected. Environmental determinants of health were knocked down by the pandemic. Healthcare systems, individual lives, and societies have been disrupted by the events of 2020.

The pandemic, the individual, and the community

The pandemic has not only increased the global burden of disease by making people sick and requiring medical attention, but it has also aggravated other pressers that increase that global burden.

The stay-at-home orders, curfews, and lockdown measures enforced in numerous cities for months at a time have created new habits linked to sedentary lifestyles, where most youths are spending time online and in front of TVs more than ever before, relying almost exclusively on screens for entertainment. These habits will probably remain in those youth's lives after the pandemic and require great awareness and public health efforts to return to pre-pandemic levels. These habits are linked to many non-communicable diseases, like heart disease, obesity, type 2 diabetes, and impaired vision.

Moreover, COVID-19 drastically raised domestic violence rates. This has taken societies years back in terms of gender-based violence programmes and other safeguarding and protection programmes. All that has left the "new normal" with a plethora of preventive and curative public health issues will require more funding to be handled in the future.

The pandemic and the health system

According to the WHO, healthcare services treating non-communicable diseases were disrupted in many countries, especially in the Global South. Many people chose not to undergo elective surgeries during the pandemic, for reasons related to the economy, physical distancing, and concerns over viral transmission within health facilities.

The scarcity of elective surgeries in 2020 will cause an acute boost in the number of surgeries undertaken after the virus subsides. This disruption will cause three major shift in the healthcare system: (1) it will cause a greater need for quality and efficiency in health services and will, in turn, increase health costs. (2) it will cause a greater need for health workers, especially nursing and community health workers leading to larger funding needs. Finally, (3) it will require more innovation, and while innovation does not mean technology, this will still mean increased spending on technological advancements, especially in Third World countries.

The pandemic and the environment

All of that mentioned previously will lead to a spiral of healthcare costs. Although it has been a long-standing problem, the increase in extensive healthcare costs will drive health policies towards more government spending on developing, recruiting, training, retaining healthcare workers, adding hospital beds, and other public health programmes. This increase in funding will cause a greater portion of government budgets to go to the healthcare sector, causing other sectors like the environment to return to a lower priority.

The pandemic has highlighted the relationship between humankind and its surrounding. It showed the disparities between sub-populations of the same country. Nevertheless, more importantly, it showed inefficiencies in pre-existing policy infrastructure significant, especially in health.

Since the early 2000s, the WHO had been attempting to measure and compare health systems through econometric principles usually used for factory production-measuring all health outcomes in terms of government spending on healthcare and minimal regard to socio-economic determinants of health. As a result, the "healthcare system efficiency" was only the "cost of care", and those most affected by the pandemic are the systems praised most for their efficiency and for lessening their government spending and the number of health workers.

The events of the year 2020 have shed light on the true meaning of healthcare efficiency: having fewer doctors on payrolls and spending less on health does not mean the state's health system is performing better. In production factories, the less spent per operation, the better the efficiency.

In healthcare, a dollar spent on low-quality care is much worse than 10 dollars spent on high-quality care, because low quality means a poorer quality of life and more burdens on the system in the future.

Environmental governance will always be a lower priority than healthcare until global authorities bridge the gap between the social, economic, and environmental determinants of health and the healthcare system's effectiveness.

Healthcare spending and pollution

Limited empirical evidence has been shown on the causality between environmental pollution and healthcare spending. The resulting causality between CO_2 emissions and health expenditures is attributed to air pollution, which has shown to be causative of many respiratory conditions.

However, a bidirectional causality exists between CO_2 emissions and economic growth and between health expenditures and economic growth (Chaabouni et al., 2016).

Healthcare spending and economic growth

A bidirectional causal relationship also exists between healthcare spending and economic growth. Studies show that increased healthcare spending per capita improves people's health and well-being, thus leading to better economic growth (Raghupathi & Raghupathi, 2020). Also, states with flourishing economies can afford to spend more on the health of their people. However, healthcare expenditure is a peculiar indicator, in that it usually tracks the spending of governments on health services).

Measuring healthcare spending is heavily reliant on the health policy in place. For example, low government spending on healthcare can be deemed efficient, since reducing healthcare costs is a priority for most states. However, low healthcare spending per capita can, in some developing countries, also mean that citizens are covering healthcare costs as out-of-pocket payments, which can in some cases reach 80% of the health bill, and drive citizens below the poverty line, an indicator of a failed health system (Raghupathi & Raghupathi, 2020).

Pollution and economic growth

Another bidirectional causal relationship is between economic growth and environmental pollution. Many studies in different fields have proven that economic advancement can be a precursor of high pollution indexes. However, others found evidence against this hypothesis (Ozturk et al., 2016).

Pollution is a significant driver of environmental destruction. It is mainly caused by the combustion of carbon-based fossil fuels to operate machines, and generate electricity, among other purposes. The by-product of this combustion is CO_2 gas which is then released into the air. Due to the large volume of CO_2 being exerted into the atmosphere, the planet's temperature is gradually rising.

Another driver of environmental degradation is the un-sustainability of agricultural practices. When executed with no regard for their effects on the environment, agricultural practices can lead to soil erosion and sediments in rivers. It can also lead to desertification, water pollution, and the contamination of rivers and seas with chemicals.

The effects of humankind on the environment are also evident by the rise of the global sea level and ocean acidification. After the global temperature rose, water from melting ice increased ocean water level and caused the rise of sea level by 1.7 mm/year during the twentieth century. Ocean acidification is the consequence of the oceans' absorption of the human-made CO_2 emissions. The oceans have absorbed around 30% of emissions caused by humans, which can have catastrophic ramifications on marine life.

Sustainable development

Sustainable development was seen as an alternative solution that preserves the environment without sacrificing economic development. The feasibility of economic growth without environmental destruction has become evident over the last few years, as some believe there can be a "de-growth phase" whereby the environment is preserved, but social efficiency and standards of quality of life are maintained.

Ecologists and economists disagree on whether it is feasible to preserve or even improve environmental impact while sustaining economic growth, with the former believing that it cannot be done, and the latter suggesting the following methods to achieve such a symbiotic relationship between the economy and the environment.

Hence, environmental sustainability ensures synergy between economic growth and the environment. It follows many principles, such as shifting to renewable resources, decreasing pollutants, targeting welfare instead of GDP inside the states, and creating long-term strategies to protect ecosystems.

Shifting to renewable energy

Renewable energy has become cheaper than other, more harmful energy-production sources (Kretchmer, 2020).

Including social cost

It is resourceful to include the external cost (e.g. carbon tax) in the price. If the payable taxes are equal to the full external cost, it will create a strong incentive to promote economic growth.

Environment as a public good

National authorities can protect and sustain the environment through implementing public policies that preserve natural resources, limit the external costs, and ensure sustainable development.

48 *Effective environmental governance*

Embrace quality of life

Economics can add other indicators to the economic progress, i.e. the quality of life and environmental indicators.

Technological investments

Much of today's new technology is leaning towards using high-efficiency and low-emissions strategies, such as LED lights, and electric cars instead of those relying on fuel combustion.

Climate change

Perhaps one of the most prominent consequences of human damage to the environment is climate change. As discussed earlier, the planet's average temperature is increasing, and global sea levels are rising. These changes can have devastating effects on the lives and livelihoods of millions around the globe and alter our economic future.

The "Intergovernmental Panel on Climate Change" (IPCC) has confirmed the Earth's temperature is indeed getting warmer and that this increase ranges between 1.1 and 6.4 degrees Celsius. Climate change will have catastrophic consequences for Third World countries, aggravating poverty, diseases, conflicts, and instability (Ha & Dhakal, 2013).

Effective environmental governance models can amplify the capability of economic systems to alleviate, adapt, and respond to the negative impacts of climate change. As discussed in Chapter 1, environmental tensions may aggravate governance challenges related to security, violence, and poverty.

Historically, combating climate change came in two forms: mitigation and adjustment. Mitigation refers to the attempts to reduce the emission of greenhouse gases to lessen the rate of climate change. Adjustment is designed to lessen the harmful acts and increase nature resilience to recover from the damage caused by climate change.

Ecosystem degradation

An ecosystem science definition entails an ecological community consisting of different populations of organisms that live together in a particular habitat. It is a geographic region where human beings, nature, climate, animals, and landscape work together to form Earth's life. Simply put, it is a group of living organisms existing and interacting together in a specific neighbourhood.

"The Millennium Ecosystem Assessment" which was initiated in 2001 by the UN Secretary-General Kofi Annan "to assess the consequences of ecosystem" found that

Over the past 50 years, humans have changed ecosystems more rapidly and extensively than in any comparable period of time in human history, largely to meet rapidly growing demands for food, fresh water, timber, fiber and fuel. This has resulted in a substantial and largely irreversible loss in the diversity of life on Earth.

(Millennium Ecosystem Assessment, 2005)

From an economic development perspective, this degradation has led to growth, well-being, and better quality of life. Nevertheless, that was done unsustainably, as it caused irreversible outcomes, and may cause diseases, shortness of water supply, and climate change.

One of the significant challenges resulting from ecosystem degradation is the destruction of biodiversity; for the loss of any species will cause damage and harmful consequences for nature.

Natural resources and waste management

Due to the increase in the utilisation of natural resources for production and the boost in consumption, significant adverse impacts have been realised. The direct environmental consequences on the depletion of resources may include pollution, desertification, freshwater shortages, and increase in poverty, instability, and environmental conflicts.

Technology and science transformed the whole world's perspectives towards waste, as it is now seen as having several characteristics. Waste was an unwanted by-product of industry and a cause for pollution and environmental degradation, but it has now become a source of energy and production.

So, waste management policies consist of reducing waste, reusing, recycling, recovering, producing energy, and disposal. However, waste management activities may cause environmental consequences as well, i.e. methane emissions from waste treatment systems, air pollution, and greenhouse gas emissions.

The 3R (Reduce, Reuse, and Recycle) initiative was promoted as the best way to effectively use resources while ensuring both environmental conservation and economic growth. It can reduce greenhouse emissions, while encouraging sustainable resource usage, and the promotion of highly efficient resource circulation. Two out of three elements of this initiative (2R = Reduce and Reuse) are considered high priority for development (Yano, 2015).

Even as waste prevention reduces negative environmental impacts, the recycling processes also have environmental effects; in most cases the overall impacts avoided by recycling and recovery are more significant than those incurred in the recycling processes (Waste & Resources Action Programme (WRAP), 2006).

International environmental governance: key challenges

Environmental governance has faced many key challenges on the international and national levels.

At the international level

Lack of shared vision among different stakeholders.
Inconsistency and fragmentation; each body follows its own agenda.
Lack of cooperation between diverse actors and stakeholders.
Lack of coordination between environmental organisations.
Insufficient global agreements.
Lack of enforcement capabilities.
Lack of coherence which leads to inefficiency.
Stakeholders' coalitions.
Non-sustainable funding.

At the national level

Unresolved tensions between economic development and environmental protection.
Insufficient commitment, implementation, and compliance.
Inability to influence public opinion due to time lag between human action and environmental effect.
Lack of gender and intergenerational equity.

Lack of government capacity to satisfy environmental obligations:

- Lack of integration of sector policies.
- Inadequate institutional capacities.
- Ill-defined priorities.
- Unclear objectives.

Towards a better international environmental governance

The Road to Reform needs consistency, perseverance, and cooperation between various stakeholders to fulfil four objectives as presented by

Nathan J. Bennett and Terre Satterfield: (1) effective governance, (2) equitable governance, (3) responsive governance, and (4) robust governance (Bennett & Terre, 2018). The main objective of "effectiveness" seeks to keep the system's resilience and functions; while "equitable" means that the policies, procedures, and outcomes are fair and leave no one behind. "Responsive governance" encourages the right adjustments when needed. "Robust governance" takes all the needed measures to keep society's endurance and performance and cope with diverse challenges.

Mainly, we can designate some principles for enhancing the International Environmental Governance System:

a) Strengthening the UNEP through comprehensive mandate and better financial support.
b) Engaging in "multilateral diplomacy" to facilitate cooperation and coordination between different stakeholders at international and national levels and between civil society, public, and private sectors (*refer to Case Study 4.2*).
c) Boosting efficiency through policies that avoid overlapping and duplication.
d) Increasing consistency and coherence between international environmental governance stakeholders by building a more integrated structure.
e) Mounting responsiveness by setting reasonable time frames for the institutions to respond to the actors' needs.
f) Becoming consent-oriented by designing policies that consider respecting different interests within the whole community to reach a broad consensus.
g) Maintaining equity and applying inclusive policies to serve the whole community, especially the most vulnerable and minority groups.
h) Increasing effectiveness through balancing the needs of society, use of resources, and environmental concerns.
i) Taking responsibilities: governments, private sector, and civil society organisations must take responsibility for the actions and decisions they make.

Case Study 4.2: multilateral diplomacy: forest conservation

In the last half-century, the world has witnessed an increase in the number of democratic states. In parallel, civil societies and NGOs have been on the rise, coupled with the increasing need for peoples to be involved in politics. Despite their questionable transparency and accountability, people had been actively engaging with causes raised by NGOs.

NGOs have become part of the reality of multilateral diplomacy. Nowadays, NGO members, scientists, and private sector experts engage directly in diplomatic activities and perform diplomats' functions: represent their institutions, exchange information, negotiate and provide advices for governments (Aviel, 2005).

Multi stakeholders have been able to exert pressure on governments to change internal policies and regulations, discuss issues beyond state boundaries, and often succeed. Negotiations' outcomes on the international trade in "The International Tropical Timber Organization" 1987 is one example.

"The European environmental NGOs network" (ECOROPA) launched a lobbying campaign to raise awareness of the cultural and ecological damage in the tropical forests caused by industrial development. Press articles, expert columns, and documentaries raised awareness on the ecological consequences of forest production industry, and the high deforestation rates, particularly in tropical countries.

The campaign succeeded to make the United Nations General Assembly hold an emergency special session on tropical deforestation, in September 1989.

Forest negotiations took place under the patronage of the "Commission on Sustainable Development", leading to the publication of "proposals for action" on forests in 1997 and 2000, and eventually led to the creation of the "United Nations Forum on Forests".

Conflict of interest between the States over the framing of deforestation issues lead to a divide. While the Global North considered deforestation to be a global issue, a group of 77 developing countries – coined the G77 – claimed sovereignty over their forest resources, viewing the issue as a national one.

The NGOs themselves witnessed a divide. Some NGOs lobbied towards the strict protection of indigenous peoples' rights in the convention, while others thought that ratifying forest conventions should be avoided.

Most environmental experts and scientists shared a perspective on the pressing need to halt and reverse deforestation in all of the planet's regions. They also contended the need for reforestation to reproduce the original natural forest conditions as closely as possible and that forest management should be ecologically sustainable and socially responsible over the long term (Humphreys, 2004).

NGOs can utilise intergovernmental disputes benefiting from individual delegations' preferences to advance their agenda. They lobbied with the Global South for indigenous peoples' rights to live in forests and realise customary and tribal knowledge of peoples as a part of their right to self-determination and heritage preservation. Others lobbied with Global North delegations to include text on participation, women's rights, indigenous heritage, and many others.

Lobbying, expert interference, and pressure from media and civil societies resulted in recognition of the "inequitable land tenure pattern" in the forest convention.

With pressure exerted from different actors, delegates included an article in the forest-related principles "to promote those land tenure arrangements that serve as incentives for the sustainable management of forests" (United Nations, 1992) (, Principle 5). In the absence of other actors, the delegates would not have had any incentive to condemn the political and economic powers owning most of the land.

Bibliography

Aviel, J.F., 2005. NGOs and International Affairs. In J. Muldoon Jr., J. Aviel, R. Reitano & E. Sullivan, eds. *Multilateral Diplomacy and the United Nations Today*. 2nd ed. Boulder, CO: Westview Press, pp. 159–172.

Bennett, N.J. & Terre, S., 2018. Environmental governance: A practical framework to guide design, evaluation, and analysis. *Conservation Letters*, 11(6). [Online] Available at: https://conbio.onlinelibrary.wiley.com/doi/full/10.1111/conl.12600 [Accessed 30 November 2020].

Chaabouni, S., Zghidi, N. & Ben Mbarek, M., 2016. On the Causal Dynamics Between CO2 Emissions, Health Expenditures and Economic Growth. *Sustainable Cited and Society*, 22, pp. 184–191.

Ha, H. & Dhakal, T.N., 2013. *Governance Approaches to Mitigation of and Adaptation to Climate Change in Asia*. London: Palgrave Macmillan.

Humphreys, D., 2004. Redefining the Issues: NGO Influence on International Forest Negotiations. *Global Environmental Politics*, 4(2), pp. 51–74.

International Institute for Sustainable Development, 2006. *Global Environmental Governance: A Reform Agenda*. [Online] Available at: https://sustainabledevelopment.un.org/index.php?page=view&type=400&nr=195&men [Accessed 20 August 2020].

Kretchmer, H., 2020. *World Economic Forum*. [Online] Available at: www.weforum.org/agenda/2020/06/renewable-energy-cheapercoal/#:~:text=Many%20new%20renewable%20energy%20projects,power%20deals%20signed%20in%202019. [Accessed 28 August 2020].

Millennium Ecosystem Assessment, 2005. *Overview of the Millennium Ecosystem Assessment*. [Online] Available at: www.millenniumassessment.org/en/About.html [Accessed 29 November 2020].

Ozturk, I., Usama, A.-M. & Saboori, B., 2016. Investigating the Environmental Kuznets Curve Hypothesis: The Role of Tourism and Ecological Footprint. *Environmental Science and Pollution Research*, 23, pp. 1916–28.

Pinner, D., Rogers, M. & Samandari, H., 2020. Addressing Climate Change in a Post-Pandemic World. *McKinsey Quarterly*, 7 April.

Raghupathi, V. & Raghupathi, W., 2020. Healthcare Expenditure and Economic Performance: Insights From the United States Data. *Frontiers in Public Health*, 8, p. 156.

Savage, J.M., Hudson, M.D. & Osborne, P.E., 2020. The Challenges of Establishing Marine Protected Areas in South East Asia. In J. Humphreys & R. Clark, eds. *Marine Protected Areas: Science, Policy and Management*. UK, Oxford: Elsevier, pp. 343–359.

United Nations, 1992. *Statement of Principles for the Sustainable Management of Forests*. Rio de Janeiro: United Nations General Assembly.

Waste & Resources Action Programme (WRAP), 2006. *Environmental Benefits of Recycling. An International Review of Life Cycle Comparisons for Crucial Materials in the UK Recycling Sector*. [Online] Available at: www.wrap.org.uk/content/environmental-benefits-recycling [Accessed 29 November 2020].

Yano, J., 2015. Waste Prevention Indicators and their Implications from the Life Cycle Perspective: A Review. *Journal of Material Cycles and Waste Management*, 18(1), pp. 38–50.

Conclusion
The need for environmental diplomats

"Humans are intergenerational animals".

– Unknown

Case Study 5.1: Environmental diplomacy through technical training at US embassies

Michael Ginsberg

Technical training not only ameliorates immediate issues but can also engender new attitudes, approaches, and even cultures within an organisation. Over the past five years, I have had the privilege of realising a technical training programme for American Embassies from West Africa to South America in building systems science, renewable energy, and preventative maintenance.

Through the training, we address immediate needs, such as reducing equipment failure and saving money, but we also raise awareness of solar and wind energy and the principles of sustainability.

As a symbol for the United States in other countries, American Embassies are a vessel for our values. By training staff in clean energy, we articulate our dedication to environmental protection. Mitigating climate change is an all-hands effort. It requires a common vernacular and knowledge base across all levels of an organisation. While ambassadors and political leaders set the vision, engineers, technicians, and facility managers do the hard work of implementing it.

There are many practical considerations. In Dakar, Senegal, we taught best practices in solar cleaning and maintenance, and the facilities team doubled the output of a large solar photovoltaic array. Many facilities integrate a solar array with a diesel generator.

56 Conclusion

> However, when in islanded mode, the variable output of a PV array forces diesel generators to rapidly fluctuate their supply and operate at low loads. At low loads, generators perform inefficiently due to incomplete combustion and reduced life. Through the training, we shared a strategy of using a hybrid controller to optimise the solar and generator output.
>
> We also taught staff how to perform energy audits and verify energy savings from more efficient HVAC systems. Past attendees have gone on to help design solar arrays for embassies and even install solar and wind turbines on their own homes.
>
> Through this training, we equipped the technical experts at US Embassies with the knowledge and skills to decarbonise our global footprint. As one of the largest contributors to greenhouse gas emissions, choosing to build and operate net zero facilities sends a strong message of solidarity with global environmental accords, such as the Paris Climate Agreement.

Michael's case has shown how diplomats in various US missions are being professionalised to build environmental knowledge, even in the technical aspects. This takes us to what Hass argued more than 20 years ago that science and scientists are shapers of the world. However, we can add to Hass argument that in our rationalist world order, it is essential to start professionalising diplomats to become "expert diplomats" in the environmental sphere.

Expert diplomats are defined as "professionals with advanced training in one or more various sciences who are authorised to make politically or legally binding decisions on regime actors". However, the notion of this expertise should not omit the political nature of international negotiations. In other words, governments should train their expert diplomats to act not just upon their scientific knowledge but also upon their political and diplomatic understanding (Lakoff, 1979).

Generally, expert diplomats or, in our case, "Environmental Diplomats" play a vital role in the pre-negotiation phase (Auer, 1998). They collectively work with the negotiating parties to define problems, address challenges, and prepare a shared space for the negotiation itself.

Nevertheless, they must be known for framing the negotiation's subjects from a technical perspective. Although their role in the negotiations' political aspect is minimal, their job is vital on the advisory aspect.

When it comes to the actual negotiations, scientists tend to stay out of political discussions. However, this is a generalist approach to understanding

Conclusion 57

their behaviour; some must assert that some States empower environmental diplomats to engage in the formal phase of negotiations actively. Amid the urgent need for proactive environmental policies, governments should start forming professional cultures to facilitate the emergence of experts' negotiation culture in environmental diplomacy. This professional culture should be comprehensive because it should include various stakeholders, lawyers, engineers, and other professional networks to form a technical-political "milieu" for environmental diplomats actively.

While a professional culture must be comprehensive in its content, it should always be global. An Environmental Diplomat should approach any environmental issue with a globalist perception. In traditional diplomacy, diplomats are trained to incline towards the national interest of their states. However, environmental diplomats should protect their state's national interest and look beyond it to foresee environmental topics as convergent issues that touch the whole universe and affect all nations.

Previous chapters in this book have shown how environmental diplomacy as a professional and academic field has developed over time. While this sphere is in linear progress, the role of diplomats is nearly absent. The urgency of acting towards protecting the environment makes us push for establishing "environmental diplomats" as a "career". This career should be linked to social and political construction in which the diplomatic factor is not replaced, but it complements the work of other diplomatic agents.

When addressing climate change diplomacy, we think of the "United Nations Framework Convention on Climate Change" (UNFCCC). While environmental diplomats should have a deeper understanding of the UNFCCC, they must also learn how to break down negotiation deadlocks. However, most of the training provided on this matter treat climate change diplomacy from the UNFCCC perspective only. There is less training provided on urbanism, cities diplomacy, and NGO diplomacy.

Private associations and NGOs usually organise training sessions on issues other than climate change. They partner with various stakeholders, including foreign affairs offices, to facilitate workshops and training sessions on various social and environmental issues.

For instance, the German Federal Office has partnered with *Global Diplomacy Lab* to organise special lab sessions on more "inclusive and agile formats of diplomacy issues". Their lab topics include gender diplomacy, cities diplomacy, and climate change diplomacy. While this project sounds promising in terms of membership and topics, other foundations such as *DiploFoundation* have not yet tackled environmental or climate change diplomacy profoundly in any of its workshops and courses.

Nevertheless, *DiploFoundation* created a public online community called "Diplo's Climate Change Community" to reach everyone interested in climate change. Thus, it is not technically oriented towards a specific category of diplomats engaged in climate change diplomacy only. Most of the training provided regarding environmental diplomacy tackles a macro-perspective of climate change.

On the governmental level, specialised schools in France such as *"Ecole Nationale d'administration"* provide specialised training on cities diplomacy, environmental protection from a regulatory perspective, EU negotiations, and much more. These executive short training pieces are not sufficient enough for mastering environmental diplomacy. What is needed is a consistent interdisciplinary training programme for environmental diplomats that would provide them with extensive knowledge and niche, at the same time, to reinforce their expertise in this sphere. An environmental diplomat should speak with an expert and a political voice at once (Loriol, 2009).

On the transnational level, the European External Action Service has voiced its interest in building a homogeneous EU foreign policy regarding pressing issues such as climate change. The preliminary step to building a unified EU foreign policy starts with trained skills diplomats that can reach some agreement between member states' divergent opinions. This mission can be done through the European Diplomatic Programme (EDP) that aims to promote diplomatic awareness concerning a unique European dimension of diplomacy (Frattini, 2010). However, the same problem persists; the *"Ecole Nationale d'administration"* and EDP training sessions are very brief and cannot cover all the training needs. EDP training sessions last around 14 days (Actimage, 2021)

Finally, an inter-diplomatic-scientific collaboration is needed to conceptualise new concepts such as *global challenges*, *risk*, and *danger* that could be considered basic scientific and political thinking vocabulary in environmental/climate issues.

As Pierre Bourdieu said, relativity in a definition can lead to a non-conformity of the word. Defining global challenges gives a shape and spirit to the environmental concept itself. Most of the time, non-conformity is linked to defining these concepts from a Western perspective. Thus, any conceptualisation should not deepen the asymmetrical perceptions between the Global South and the Global North, leading to further interpretations and uncertainties.

To conclude, environmental diplomats should engage in an ethical and philosophical debate when it comes to taking moral actions. Being a "technocratic" or expert diplomat is not enough vis-à-vis this intergenerational field that requires a sense of moral awareness and responsibility. This moral consciousness must be embedded with the diplomats' understanding of how their actions can influence future generations as well as predecessors. In a much simple manner, any diplomatic action must be taken not just from an interest-based perspective but also from an intergenerational justice and equity prism.

Bibliography

Actimage, 2021. *Short Specialized International Cycles, ENA*. Available at: /eng/Europe-and-International/Programmes-de-formation/cisap [Accessed 31 January 2021].

Auer, 1998. Colleagues or Combatants? Experts as Environmental Diplomats. *International Negotiation*, 3(2), pp. 267–287. https://doi.org/10.1163/15718069820 848210.

Frattini, F., 2010. The European External Action Service: A Look into EU Diplomat Training. *European View*, 9(2), pp. 219–227. https://doi.org/10.1007/s12290-010-0134-2.

Lakoff, S.A., 1979. Scientists and World Order: The Uses of Technical Knowledge in International Organizations. Ernst B. Haas, Mary Pat Williams, Don Babai. *Isis*, 70(3), pp. 445–446. https://doi.org/10.1086/352293.

Loriol, M., 2009. La carrière des diplomates français: entre parcours individuel et structuration collective. *SociologieS*, pp. 1–18.

Index

3R (Reduce, Reuse, and Recycle) initiative 49
"2030 Agenda" for Sustainable Development (2016) 18

advocacy coalitions 30
aerosols 15
Agenda 21 15–16, 23
Agenda 2030 18
air pollution 49; carbon dioxide (CO_2) emissions 16, 45; health expenditures due to 45; international law on 13
Aldrin, Philippe 30–31
allowed pollution, quotas of 20
ambassadors 2, 55
Amsterdam Treaty (1997) 26
Annan, Kofi 49
anthropogenic interference, with the climate system 15
anti-poverty movement 17
aristocrats 2
associative diplomacy 8
Astroturf 25, 35

balance of power 2, 5, 22
Ban Ki-moon 18, 34
Berny, Nathalie 26
biodiversity, destruction of 49
biofuels 34
Bourdieu, Pierre 28, 37, 58
Brick, Patrick ten 33
Brown, Lester 4
Brundtland, Harlem 14
Brundtland Report (1987) 14–15
Byzantine Empire 1

carbon dioxide (CO_2) emissions 16, 45, 47
Caring for the Earth: A Strategy for Sustainable Living (1991) 14
chlorofluorocarbons (CFCs) 15
citizen movements, rise of 31
civic interest groups 30
civil societies 8, 37, 51
civil society organisations 9, 29, 51
Civil War in Syria *see* Syrian conflict
climate change 4, 18, 48; diplomacy 57–58; dispute over 21; fight against 26; mitigation of 48, 55; *see also* global warming
climate-related security concerns 4
coalition negotiation 8
Cold War 2, 4
Commission on Sustainable Development (CSD) 16, 52
common but differentiated responsibility, principle of 20
communication technologies 3
communities of states 3
compartmentalisation of markets, between European countries 30–31
Congress of Vienna (1815) 2
Convention on Biological Diversity (1992) 15
cooperation, principle of 19
COVID-19 pandemic: effects on lessening pollution 42; and the environment 41–45; environment's silver lining 42–44; global burden of 44; and health system 44; human and economic costs of 43; outbreak

Index 61

of 42; physical distancing 42; stay-at-home orders 44; viral transmission within health facilities 44
customary international law 13

decision-making procedures and policies 17, 28
deforestation, rate of 52
democratic deficit 28, 31, 36
DiploFoundation 57–58
diplomacy 1–3, 58
diplomatic agenda, augmentation of 3, 57
diplomatic customs, in Byzantine Empire 1
diplomatic practices, regulation of 2
diplomatic relations: environment in 3–4; norms and customs of 2; Vienna Convention on Diplomatic Relations (1961) 2
Diplo's Climate Change Community 57

Earth Summit in Rio (1972–1992) 15–16
Ecole Nationale d'administration (France) 58
ecological community 48
ecological security 4
economic crisis 42
economic development 19, 21–22, 47, 49–50
economic diplomacy 7
economic growth 15; healthcare spending and 46; pollution and 46–47
economic organisations and lobbies 30
economic recession 6
ecosystems: degradation of 48–49; strategies to protect 47
environment: benefits and risks of decisions on 19–20; COVID-19 pandemic and 41–45; in diplomatic relations 3–4; effects of humankind on 46; quality of life and 41; relation with national security 4
environmental advocacy, at international and regional levels: in Europe 31, 36–37; European Environmental Bureau (EEB) 31–33; Greenpeace 33–34; United Nations Sustainable Development Solutions Network (UNSDSN) 34–36
environmental conflicts: as challenge for states' foreign policies 7; due to abundance of natural resources 4; East and West Africa conflicts 5; globalisation 6; human migration 6; narratives on 4–6; population growth 5–6; relation with natural resource scarcity 5; unequal resource distribution 6
environmental cooperation, at the regional and global levels 14
environmental customary laws 12
environmental damage 22
environmental degradation 43; harmful impacts of 15; measures to prevent 20; ozone depletion 13; problem of 13
environmental diplomacy 4, 7; proliferation of IGOs and 8; through technical training at US embassies 55–56
environmental diplomats 56–57, 58
environmental disputes 13
environmental governance 7, 9, 45, 48; decision-making powers 40; definition of 40; effectiveness of 41; environmental policy priority areas 41–50; indicators of "good governance" 41; at international level 50; key challenges 50–51; at national level 50; principles of 40–41; Road to Reform 50–51
environmental habitats, loss of 41
environmental harm: duty to prevent 19; trans-boundary 18
environmental justice 32
environmental non-governmental organisations (ENGOs) 8, 25; advocacy of 29–30, 37; Brussels 9; challenges faced by 25; degree of politicisation in 29; features of 25; interest groups within the EU 28–29; lobbying by 29–30, 37; non-Brussels 9; organisational charters of 25
environmental policy priority areas 41–50; climate change 48; ecosystem degradation 48–49; natural resources and waste management 49–50; quality of life and environment

41–47; shifting to renewable energy 47–48; sustainable development 47
environmental pollution 41; as driver of environmental destruction 46; and economic growth 46–47; and healthcare spending 45–46; high pollution indexes 46
environmental protection 15, 18; application of IEL for 21; economic compensation for 22; international cooperation for 19; processes of 40
environmental risks: precautionary principle on 19–20; sustainable policies in response to 7
environmental security 4; COVID-19 pandemic and 43; and peace-building 7
environmental sustainability 47
environmental treaties 4, 12, 22
Eric, Andrija 35
EU Green Diplomacy Network 8
Eurobarometer 31
Europe: civil society 29, 30–31; diplomacy 2; environmental law 26–27; environmental NGOs network (ECOROPA) 52; institutions 28, 30–31, 36–37; political system 28
European Commission 26, 30–31, 35; formation of 30; transparency register 28; use of European civil society by 31
European Council 30
European Diplomatic Programme (EDP) 58
European Environmental Bureau (EEB) 31–33; energy decarbonisation strategy within Green Deal 32–33; founding of 32
European External Action Service 58
European Parliament 29–32, 36–37
European Policy Network 35
European Union (EU): decision-making processes 32; democratic deficit 31; democratic functioning of 29; Environmental Bureau 9; environmental policy 36; formation of 30; Green Deal 25–26, 32, 33, 34, 36; interest groups 27–29; lobbying strategies 30; representative groups 27
expert diplomats 9, 56, 58

food: insecurity 6; security 4, 6, 17
foreign ministries' system 2
forests: conservation 9; multilateral diplomacy in conservation 51–53; production industry 52; rights to live in 53
fossil fuels, carbon-based 43, 46
Future We Want, The 17

G77 countries 52
Global Diplomacy Lab 57
global environmental protection 40
global equity 32
globalisation 6
Global North 52–53, 58
Global South 44, 53, 58
global temperature, rise in 18, 46–47
global warming 16, 18; *see also* climate change
government-to-government diplomacy 2–3
GREEN 10 (environmental NGOs) 32
Green Deal 25–26, 32–33, 34, 35, 36
greenhouse emissions 16, 49, 56; European "Green Deal" for reducing 26; mitigation of 48
Greenpeace 9, 37; energy decarbonisation strategy within Green Deal 34; European unit 33
Guide to Effective Lobbying of the European Parliament 29
Guterres, António 4

healthcare spending 41; COVID-19 pandemic and 44; and economic growth 46; and pollution 45–46
healthcare systems 44; costs of 45; COVID-19 pandemic and 44; and pollution 45–46; quality and efficiency in 44–45; spending in 41; treating non-communicable diseases 44
heritage preservation, right to 53
high politics, notion of 3–4, 9, 29
high pollution indexes 46
Hocking, Brian 3
Ho-Won, Jeong 6
humans/human: dignity 18; migration 6; poverty 7; security 3, 7
HVAC systems 56

Index 63

indigenous peoples 53
industrial revolution 2
intergenerational: equity 19; justice 59
Intergovernmental Panel on Climate Change (IPCC) 48
inter-institutional balance 30
International Convention for the Regulation of Whaling 21
International Environmental Governance System 40, 50, 51
International Environmental Law (IEL): ad hoc treaties 13; application of 21–22; Article 21 of 14; bilateral agreements between states 13; challenges faced by 22–23; compliance with 22; development and application of 19; development of 14, 16; enforcement of 23; environmental regulations 21; first generation 13; fourth generation 16–18; history of 12–18; implementation of 23; principles of 18–20; rules of 20; science-economy trade-offs and 21–22; scientific foundation of 21; second generation 13–14; as soft law 20–21; stages of evolution 12; third generation 14–16; weaknesses of 20–21
international environmental organisations: creation of 13; initiation of 14
international governmental organisations (IGOs) 2–3, 8
International Institute for Sustainable Development 40
International Tropical Timber Organization 52
intra-generational equity 19

job opportunities 18
Johannesburg Declaration (2004) 17

Kyoto Protocol (1997) 16

land tenure arrangements 53
law of nations, relating to ambassadors 2
Leyen, Van Der 32–33
LIFE programme 25
Lisbon Treaty (2009) 26
low politics, notion of 4

Maastricht Treaty (1992) 26
man–nature relationship 4
marine environment 14
marine living resources, protection of 14
methane emissions 49
Michel, Hélène 27–28, 31
Millennium Development Goals (MDGs) 16–18
Millennium Ecosystem Assessment (2001) 49
Montevideo Programme (1981) 14
Montreal Protocol (1987) 12, 15, 21
moral consciousness 58
multilateral diplomacy 2–3, 51; effectiveness of 9; for forest conservation 51–53
multinational corporations 2

national societies, aggregation of 30
natural resources: conventions regulating 7; demand for 4; demand-induced scarcity 5; human activity consequences on 12; need to preserve and sustain the use of 19; present and future generations' rights over 19; relationship with environmental conflict 4; states' sovereignty over 18; structural scarcity 5; supply-induced scarcity 5; sustainable use of 19; utilisation of 49; and waste management 49–50
nature degradation 12
negotiations, on nature 7–9
non-communicable diseases 44
non-governmental organisations (NGOs) 2, 14, 29, 51
non-renewable resources, over-consumption of 41
non-state actors 2–3, 8, 13, 23

ocean acidification 46–47
"Our Common Future" report (1987) 14–15
ozone layer 12, 13, 15

Paris Agreement (2015) 18, 56
participatory democracy 32
peace-building 7
people's health and well-being 46
permanent diplomatic missions 2

plenipotentiaries 1
political advocacy alliances 30
"polluter pays" principle 20
population growth 5–6
precautionary principle 19–20
Principle 21, adoption of 13, 18–19
private interest groups, influence of 28, 30
problem-solving 34
public diplomacy 3

quality of life 9, 41, 45, 47, 48–49

recycling practices, rise in 4
Regional Seas Program 13
renewable energies 34; as public good 47; quality of life and 48; social cost of 47; technological investments 48
resource consumption 41
Rio+20 Conference (2012) 17
Rio Declaration (1992) 12, 23; Principle 2 of 18, 19; Principle 7 of 20; Principle 15 of 20; Principle 16 of 20; Principle 27 of 19
Rio Summit *see* Earth Summit in Rio (1972–1992)
Roman Catholic Church 1
Roman Empire 1
Rome, Treaty of 28

sea level, rise of 4, 46–48
self-determination, right to 53
Sen, B. 2
Single European Act (1986) 26
single market programme 30
social equity 15
social movement, activism of 29
social protection, for vulnerable groups 18
socio-economic determinants, of health 45
"sovereign shall make no harm" principle 18
Statement of Principles for the Sustainable Management of Forests 15
states' representative 3
state system, evolution of 2
state-to-state-only diplomacy 2
Stockholm Conference (1945–1972) 13–14

Stockholm Declaration (1972) 12, 13, 15; Principle 21 of 18, 19; Principle 24 of 19
sustainable agricultural reserves 17
sustainable development 12, 14–15, 16–17, 32, 47; Commission on Sustainable Development (CSD) 16, 52; concept of 15; integration of 14; legal elements related to 19; principle of 19; problem-solving solutions for 34; three pillars of 15
Sustainable Development Goals (SDGs): Agenda 2030 18; implementation of 35
Sustainable Development Solutions Network (SDSN) 31, 34–36
sustainable peace, concept of 7
symbiotic relationship, between the economy and the environment 47
Syrian conflict 5

Third World countries 44, 48
trade sanctions 21
traditional diplomacy 1–2, 3, 57
Trail Smelter case 13, 19
Transparency International 25

unemployment insurance 42
UNEP Draft Principles (1978) 14
unequal resource distribution 6
United Nations (UN): annual climate summit 43; Commission on Sustainable Development (CSD) 16, 17; Conference on Environment and Development (UNCED) 15, 16, 23; Convention on the Law of the Sea (UNCLOS) 14; creation of 13; Earth Summit in Rio (1972–1992) 14–15; Environment Program (UNEP) 7, 13–14, 15; Framework Convention on Climate Change (UNFCCC) 16, 18, 57; General Assembly 14, 16, 52; Millennium Declaration 16; Millennium Ecosystem Assessment (2001) 49; Principle 21, adoption of 13; Security Council 4; Stockholm Conference (1945–1972) 13–14; Sustainable Development Solutions Network (UNSDSN) 9, 34–36

Vienna Convention for the Protection of the Ozone Layer (1985) 12
Vienna Convention on Diplomatic Relations (1961) 2

waste: management 4, 49–50; treatment systems 49
water security 4
Weisbein, Julien 30
Westphalia, Treaty of 2
White Paper on European governance 31

World Charter for Nature (1982) 14
World Commission on Environment and Development (WCED) 14
World Conservation Strategy (1980) 14
World Health Organization (WHO) 42
"The World in 2050" research project 35
World Summit on Sustainable Development (2002) 17

youth bulge's narrative 5

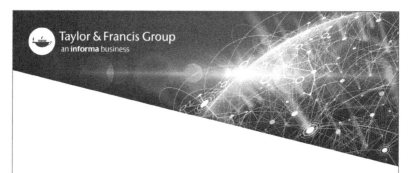